RED
HOT
KITCHEN

RED HOT KITCHEN

Classic Asian Chili
Sauces from Scratch
and Delicious Dishes
to Make with Them

DIANA KUAN

AVERY

AN IMPRINT OF PENGUIN RANDOM HOUSE
NEW YORK

AVERY

an imprint of Penguin Random House LLC
1745 Broadway
New York, New York 10019

Most Avery books are available at special quantity discounts for bulk purchase for sales promotions, premiums, fund-raising, and educational needs. Special books or book excerpts also can be created to fit specific needs. For details, write SpecialMarkets@penguinrandomhouse.com.

ISBN 9780525533528 (hardcover)
ISBN 9780525533535 (cbook)

Printed in China

10 9 8 7 6 5 4 3 2 1

Book design by Ashley Tucker

TO MY FAMILY IN MASSACHUSETTS,
PUERTO RICO, HONG KONG, AND
MAINLAND CHINA, WHO INSTILLED
IN ME AN EARLY LOVE OF FOOD
THAT IS STILL IN FULL FORCE TODAY

CONTENTS

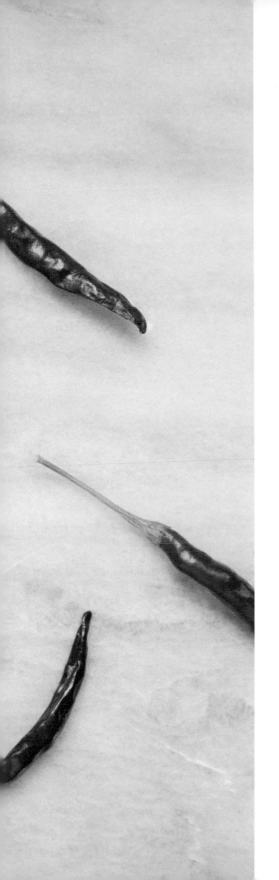

XO SAUCE DRY-FRIED
GREEN BEANS, PAGE 181

SOME LIKE IT HOT

LIKE MANY KIDS IN THE US, I DIDN'T GROW UP LOVING SPICY FOOD. My family is originally from Hong Kong and Southern China, and the food that my mom cooked at home, true to its Cantonese roots, was extremely flavorful but incorporated minimal amounts of sauces and spices. And no chilies. To most people with a Cantonese background, including my dad and grandparents, the hot sauces used in Sichuan, Hunan, and other parts of China were heavy-handed and masked the freshness of vegetables, seafood, and meat. And so our kitchen and dining room table remained chili-free.

Eating out was a different story. Despite what she cooked for us at home, my mom occasionally had a hankering for the hot stuff. When we went out to noodle shops in Boston's Chinatown, periodically a bright red bottle of Sriracha would show up on the table. While not Chinese, Sriracha from the Huy Fong brand, created by a Chinese-Vietnamese immigrant to the United States, and based on a Thai chili sauce, had become a staple in American Chinatowns by the mid-1990s. My mom loved to add a few dabs to her hand-pulled noodles, so one day I tried a few squirts on mine. The heat was so intense I almost cried. And avoided hot sauces for years after.

It wasn't until I moved to Beijing at the age of twenty-five that I started eating spicy food on a regular basis. The city was two thousand miles from Sichuan Province, but Beijingers wholeheartedly adopted the hot, numbing cuisine as their own. It wasn't uncommon to see city blocks with rows of Sichuan restaurants, one after the other, with window ads showcasing hotpots bubbling with bright red broth and signature dishes smothered with smoked chilies. Beijingers seemed to subsist primarily on Sichuan food, with local Beijing treats like boiled dumplings, hand-pulled noodles, and other street snacks to supplement the diet. And I followed suit.

Within a couple of months, I was addicted to the hot, sour, smoky flavors of Sichuan food, so much so that when I traveled to locales with less fiery foods, I went through Sichuan food withdrawal. In the two years that I lived in China, I also took periodic trips around East and Southeast Asia and, in addition to Sichuan chili oil, also became hooked on Korean gochujang, Indonesian sambal, and Japanese yuzu kosho. I also became addicted to Thailand's nam prik pao, red curry paste, sweet chili sauce, and, of course, traditional Sriracha. I even discovered that Hong Kong, home of the mild cuisine my family cooked, had its own incredibly addictive chili paste—XO sauce.

Chilies are so integral to the cuisines of many areas in Asia that it's surprising they didn't make their appearance on that continent until just a few hundred years ago. Ethnobotanists believe that chili peppers originated in Mexico, Bolivia, and Brazil, but by the fifteenth century, humans and birds (see Beak Performance, page 88) had spread them throughout South and Central America. Like tomatoes, maize, and squashes, chilies had long been an established part of most diets across the Americas, but unknown to the rest of the world until Christopher Columbus hit the Americas in the 1490s while trying to find Asia. Just as he confused the Americas for India, he also mistook chilies for black pepper (hence today these piquant plants are called both chilies and peppers).

Columbus brought chilies back to the Iberian Peninsula, where they were grown and sold as curious ornamental plants rather than as cooking ingredients. In the 1500s, Portuguese traders brought chilies to India and along the way, gained control of the spice trade in Goa. Goan cooks readily incorporated chilies into their cuisine, which already featured an abundance of spices, including black pepper, cinnamon, and cardamom. It is theorized that India, Portuguese, Indian, and Arab traders brought chilies to the Malay Peninsula, Thailand, Java and Sumatra, the Philippines, China, and Japan; later on, in the 1600s, Portuguese missionaries introduced them to Korea.

A plant that's easy to grow in a variety of climates, chilies and their culinary use spread quickly around Asia. They were also cheap, abundant, and naturally antimicrobial, so not only did they keep meat and vegetables from spoiling, but sauces made with chilies could be preserved without refrigeration.

Moving back home to New York from China, I started experimenting with making my own chili sauces. While Asian markets abound in the city and my favorite hot sauces were easy to find, I found that I preferred buying fresh chilies from the farmers' markets and tweaking chili sauces to my ideal levels of spiciness.

I've been teaching cooking classes in New York for the past ten years, creating classes on cuisines from around Asia. Over this time, I've found that the classes that sell out the fastest, and the ones most often requested for private home sessions, involve dishes that pack serious heat. I also get emails from students from outside the city who've attended classes I've taught, asking for advice on making homemade hot sauces. Sometimes they live far from an Asian grocery store. Other times, they just want to create and customize sauces using all-natural ingredients. One thing is clear: Asian hot sauces have become the next frontier for any spice fiend who enjoys DIY food projects.

So I decided to write this book, which details how to create nine of my favorite hot sauces from around Asia: sambal oelek, Sriracha, nam prik pao, Thai red curry paste, sweet chili sauce, Sichuan chili oil, XO sauce, gochujang, and yuzu kosho. In each chapter, there are also a range of traditional and experimental appetizers, main dishes, and sides to make with each sauce. Of course, this is not meant to be an encyclopedia of Asian chili sauces; just writing about the variations of sambal alone could fill volumes! Rather, this book is a celebration of the nine most versatile sauces that can be used as both a condiment and a cooking ingredient, and that also represent a broad range of geographical areas.

I should also note that for the book, some of the sauces have more of a paste-like than saucy texture. I lament that English doesn't have an all-encompassing word for "thin or thick liquid ingredient that can be used as both a condiment and cooking ingredient," like the Chinese word *jiang*. So succinct, right? To me, the textural difference between sauce and paste is so hazy, more of a gradation than a clear line, that the thicker ingredients we'll encounter here should also be considered sauces. After all, can't barbecue sauce, applesauce, and salsa be pretty thick, too?

In any case, these sauces add heat that range from a subtle kick to a scorching burn in your favorite stir-fries, appetizers, and noodle dishes. You can spend as little as 20 minutes to complete your own homemade sambal and sweet chili sauce, or wait up to 2 months to ferment gochujang the traditional way (don't worry, there's an easier version, too). The dishes you can make with the sauces include a variety of appetizers, entrees, sides, and even a few desserts, and run the gamut from traditional to globally inspired. At least half the dishes are vegetarian, and I've included vegetarian versions of sauces that traditionally have seafood or meat in them.

Enjoy these recipes, and feel free to be experimental and create your own favorite ways to use these nine hot sauces. Now that Sriracha has become a go-to condiment for just about everything we eat, and chili fiends are concocting their own signature sauces as we speak, let your imagination run wild with possibilities. Chilies have been embraced by so many cultures for good reason. They're exciting—and they make any food or cooking experiment that much more fun.

CHILI PEPPERS 101

HOW HOT CAN IT GET?

While people react differently to heat from the same chili pepper, a standardized heat range system was developed in 1912 by Wilbur Scoville to measure the levels of capsaicin, the compound in chili peppers that makes them hot. Named the Scoville Organoleptic Test, the method tests how much sugar water has to be diluted into a chili pepper mash until the heat is no longer detected to a professional taste tester. For example, a cayenne pepper mash that takes somewhere between 30,000 to 50,000 cups of sugar water to dilute until the heat can't be tasted would be labeled 30,000 to 50,000 Scoville units. (There is a range in the units because the same type of chilies can vary a lot in their spiciness depending on where they're grown and how ripe they are.) Of course, this older system was not the most precise approach, as it was subject to the heat tolerance of the taste testers.

The scale goes from 0 units (for sweet peppers and bell peppers) to well over 16 million units, the level of pure capsaicin, which thankfully no chili pepper has reached yet. Heat levels for common peppers include 2,500 to 8,000 units for jalapeños, 100,000 to 350,000 units for habaneros, and over 2 million units for the Carolina Reaper, which until May 2017 was the hottest pepper in the world. It has since been beaten out by the Dragon's Breath and Pepper X (which at over 3 million units are at levels that can severely damage your lungs and esophagus) in plant growers' seemingly endless quests for hotter peppers.

However, just measuring the spiciness doesn't tell everything about the chili. Some have heat that come on quickly and disappear, while others take time to become noticeable and linger for a long slow burn. Some heat feels like pinpricks on the lips and tongue, while others are flatter and burn at the back of the throat.

These days, capsaicin levels are determined by computer-assisted high-performance liquid chromatography, which can measure the capsaicin in the peppers without human taste testers. However, sticking to a scale familiar to chili fans, scientists still convert the results to Scoville standards to measure the heat.

ANAHEIM CHILIES

These long, thick chilies are a hybrid pepper developed in the American Southwest in the early 1900s. The flavor is bright, clean, and a little fruity. They serve as good introductions to the world of hot chilies, if you or someone you're cooking for would prefer a milder version of sambal, Sriracha, or sweet chili sauce.

KNOW YOUR CHILI PEPPER

The chart below shows the average range of Scoville units, but the actual heat of any chili pepper can vary greatly depending on many factors, including the environment, seed lineage, soil, etc.

CHILES	SCOVILLE UNITS/LENGTH	SUBSTITUTES	BEST SAUCES
ANAHEIM (sold fresh or dried)	500–2,500 6–8 inches	Fresno, jalapeño, serrano	Mild versions of sambal oelek, Sriracha, sweet chili sauce
FRESNO (sold fresh or dried)	2,500–8,500 2–3 inches	Jalapeño, Anaheim, serrano	Sambal oelek, Sriracha, sweet chili sauce, XO sauce
JALAPEÑOS (fresh) / **CHIPOTLE** (dried)	2,500–8,000 3–4 inches	Fresno, serrano, Anaheim	Sambal oelek, Sriracha, sweet chili sauce, XO sauce, yuzu kosho (takes the place of Japanese takanotsume)
GOCHU (usually sold dried and either crushed or ground)	4,000–8,000 2½–3 inches (but usually sold crushed or ground)	Ground Aleppo chilies (slightly sweeter), ground chipotle balanced with ground cayenne	Gochujang
SERRANO (sold fresh or dried)	10,000–20,000 2–3½ inches	Jalapeños, Thai spur chilies	Sambal oelek, Sriracha, sweet chili sauce. Dried serranos can be used for nam prik pao, Thai red curry paste, XO sauce, and Sichuan chili oil
THAI SPUR CHILIES/ PRIK CHEE FAH (sold fresh or dried)	5,000–30,000 3–6 inches	Fresh: serrano, Fresno, cayenne Dried: cayenne, Japonés	Nam prik pao, Thai red curry paste, XO sauce, Sichuan chili oil
JAPONÉS CHILIES (usually sold dried)	15,000–30,000 2½–3 inches	Tien Tsin, cayenne, Thai spur chilies	Nam prik pao, Thai red curry paste, XO sauce, Sichuan chili oil
CAYENNE (sold fresh or dried)	30,000–50,000 3½–8 inches	Thai spur chilies, Japonés chilies, Tien Tsin chilies	Sichuan chili oil, XO sauce, nam prik pao, Thai red curry paste
TIEN TSIN CHILIES/ CHINESE RED CHILIES (usually sold dried)	50,000–75,000 2½–3 inches	Japonés, cayenne, Thai spur chilies	Sichuan chili oil, Thai red curry paste, nam prik pao, XO sauce
BIRD'S EYE CHILIES/PRIK KEE NOO (usually sold fresh)	50,000–100,000 1–2½ inches long	Thai spur chilies, cayenne, or serrano	Mix in a few for a hotter Sriracha or sambal oelek. I don't recommend doing entire chili sauces with only bird's eye chilies (ouch!).

FRESNO CHILIES

From the outside, Fresno chilies look a lot like jalapeños. Both are about even in terms of heat level and have a crisp flavor when unripe. Fresno chilies, however, ripen faster and have a tendency to become fruitier and smokier when they turn red. They are incredibly versatile and make excellent ingredients for fresh chili sauces.

JALAPEÑOS/CHIPOTLE CHILIES

These super-versatile chilies have a moderate heat and a bright, clean flavor. They can be used as easily in Asian hot sauces as they are in Mexican or Tex-Mex cooking. (In fact, California-grown jalapeños are what go in the ubiquitous Huy Fong brand of Sriracha.) Ripe red jalapeños are more suitable for most of the chili sauces in this book because of their color and higher heat levels, though the milder unripe green jalapeños are perfect for Japanese Yuzu Kosho (page 210). Red jalapeños with white lines are at their ripest, "almost bursting at the seams" as one chili farmer told me. Fresno chilies are the best substitutes, but you can also use Anaheim chilies for less heat and serrano chilies for more intense heat. Chipotle peppers, the dried smoked versions of jalapeños, can be blended with crushed red chili flakes (cayenne) as a substitute for Korean gochugaru in a pinch.

GOCHU CHILIES

Gochu chilies are most often used in the form of gochugaru, which simply means "dried red chili flakes" or "chili powder" in Korean. It has a mild heat and smoky yet sweet spiciness. Aleppo chilies, which have a relatively mild sweet kick, are the best substitute, but they are relatively hard to find outside of specialty spice stores and Middle Eastern markets. You can also use chipotle peppers, which are made by drying and smoking ripe jalapeños, if you like a dish that is very smoky. If you'd prefer your gochugang,

ANAHEIM CHILIES

FRESNO CHILIES

JALAPEÑOS/CHIPOTLE CHILIES

GOCHU CHILIES

SERRANO CHILIES

THAI SPUR CHILIES

kimchi, or other dish with knockout spiciness, you can substitute with the same amount of cayenne, which is five to ten times spicier.

SERRANO CHILIES

If you adore store-bought Sriracha or sambal oelek but feel the sauces could be hotter, try making them at home with serrano chilies instead. Serranos are smaller than jalapeños but on average can be three times hotter. Like jalapeños, they have a bright, clean flavor when green but become slightly sweeter and hotter when they ripen.

THAI SPUR CHILIES

These skinny little chilies may cause the most confusion of any on this list. They are most frequently mixed up with Thai bird's eye chilies, which are shorter, shaped like tiny drops, and much hotter. Adding to the confusion is that growers and sellers call them many different names, including Thai chilies (which bird's eye chilies are also often called), spur chilies, Bangkok chilies, and *prik chee fah*, which translates to "chili pointing to the sky." Because up to seventy-nine different chilies are grown in Thailand and can thus be called "Thai chilies," I will refer to *prik chee fah* in this book as "Thai spur chilies." Don't despair; they are the most common types of skinny fresh chilies between three to six inches long available at Asian markets in the US. Chances are, if you're shopping stateside at an Asian market, you can easily spot the difference between them and bird's eye chilies, the other common variety in this country.

JAPONÉS CHILIES

Japonés chilies are one of the two most common dried chilies used in Chinese cooking, along with the much hotter Tien Tsin chilies, which they resemble. Japonés chilies are rusty red orange in color, with a medium heat that lingers on the tongue. Despite the name, which comes from the Spanish word for "Japanese," they are frequently used in Sichuan, Hunan, and Thai cuisines, and almost never in Japanese cooking. They are great for the times you'd prefer a medium heat (over the intense heat that Tien Tsin chilies bring) in Sichuan chili oil, Thai nam prik pao and red curry pastes, and Chinese and Thai stir-fries.

CAYENNE CHILIES

Easy to find in the US, this versatile medium-hot chili pepper is thought to be the first type brought to Asia by Portuguese traders in the 1500s. Because the size of smaller cayennes and their heat levels are roughly similar to that of Japonés chilies, Thai spur chilies, and Tien Tsin chilies, cayennes are good substitutes whenever it's difficult to find any of the aforementioned peppers. While it's possible to find them fresh, they are most often used dried, either whole, ground, or crushed into flakes. The same crushed red chili flakes we often shake on our pizza slices or roasted vegetables can be used for Asian chili sauces, pastes, and oils.

TIEN TSIN CHILIES

Pronounced "tea-an sin," these dried red peppers are also called Chinese red chilies and look almost identical to Japonés chilies. Both are used often in Chinese cooking, and the only way to tell the difference is by color (Tien Tsin are bright ruby red, whereas Japonés chilies tend to be more orangey red) and to taste them: Tien Tsin chilies are two to three times hotter than Japonés chilies. These alarmingly hot chilies can look innocent enough: They are often cooked whole for their smokiness and they accompany many Sichuan and Hunan dishes as bright red garnishes. It isn't until their seeds are unleashed (for example, crushed in a food processor for hot sauce or when some-

JAPONÉS CHILIES   TIEN TSIN CHILIES

CAYENNE CHILIES

BIRD'S EYE CHILIES

one unwittingly bites into one) that you get their full force. Much like cayenne, they are long, skinny, and they are not very complex in flavor beyond heat. Dried Tien Tsin peppers are often crushed and used to infuse Sichuan chili oil, adding a gorgeous bright red color. Chongqing Chicken (page 155) and Kung Pao Sweet Potatoes (page 161) are two examples of dishes in which smoked Tien Tsin chilies really shine.

BIRD'S EYE CHILIES

Also called Thai dragon peppers or *prik kee noo*, bird's eye chilies are among the spiciest peppers grown in Thailand. They are very tiny, usually no longer than 1½ inches, though a few varieties in California can be as long as 2½ inches. They are frequently confused with Thai spur chilies (see Thai spur chilies, page 15). They are sold both green (unripe) and red (ripe), with the red variety being a tiny bit less spicy than the green. The heat from bird's eye chilies can sneak up on you and keep building as you eat, and even linger long after you stop eating.

BE CAREFUL: WEAR RUBBER GLOVES!

It's wise to wear gloves when working with chilies, especially if you wear contact lenses. The oil and juices from the chilies and the heat chemical capsaicin can stay on your fingers for many hours and leave a stinging burn if you touch your eyes or face later. (I had several unfortunate contacts-related incidents in my early years of making chili sauces barehanded!) I keep a box of vinyl single-use gloves around for just this purpose and they work like a charm.

If you do end up with chili juices on your hands, wash them with oil-cutting dish soap, then soak them in milk or yogurt, whose protein casein neutralizes the heat. Be sure to also use oil-cutting soap to thoroughly wash your knives, cutting board, and anything else that touches the chilies.

When grinding or processing a large number of chilies, it's also important to work in a well-ventilated area, especially if you have asthma or other breathing problems.

INGREDIENTS AND EQUIPMENT

Over the past few decades, ingredients and equipment to make Asian dishes have become increasingly easier to find in the US, not just in cities but also in suburban areas and online. Use this guide to familiarize yourself with the best fresh ingredients, pantry staples, and cooking equipment for making the dishes in this book. If you can't find certain pantry staples in your area, try the resources in Where to Buy Ingredients Online (page 247).

VEGETABLES AND FRESH HERBS

BABY BOK CHOY

This member of the cabbage family is a versatile vegetable that can be used in a number of ways, from stir-frying to steaming to soups. The smaller variety of baby bok choy measures about 3 inches long, with bright white stems and dark green leaves. The larger variety (also known as Shanghai bok choy) is about 4 inches long with pale yellow stems and lighter green leaves. When buying baby bok choy, look for crisp stalks and leaves that aren't wilting.

CILANTRO

Also known as fresh coriander, this bright green herb is frequently used in Southeast Asian cooking to both heighten other flavors and cut the richness of a dish. When shopping, look for a bright green color and vibrant, unwilted leaves.

DAIKON RADISH

Sometimes called Chinese turnip, these large, long radishes have a firm white flesh and a mildly spiced bite. When buying daikon, look for firm ones that have smooth and unwrinkled skin. They are usually steamed, pickled, or braised (see Red-Cooked Beef with Daikon Radish on page 151), but can also be eaten raw in salads. Always wash and peel daikon to remove any grit that can get lodged in the outer skin. Daikon radish can be stored in the refrigerator for up to 10 days.

GALANGAL

A rhizome like ginger, galangal has a sharp citrusy, almost piney flavor. It is used in many dishes in Thai, Indonesian, and Malaysian cooking. The skin can be peeled with a metal spoon like ginger, but it is much harder inside. You can sometimes substitute ginger in a pinch, but the flavor in your dish will be mellower and less herbaceous.

SHANGHAI BABY BOK CHOY

SMALLER
BABY BOK CHOY

THAI BASIL

KAFFIR LIME LEAVES

GALANGAL

GARLIC CHIVES

These chives with long green stems and a bud-like tip have a mild garlic and onion flavor and a crisp texture. Add them to stir-fries, soups, or dumpling fillings.

GINGER

A key component in many East and Southeast Asian dishes, ginger has a clean sharp flavor that makes both seafood and meat taste fresher, and also cuts the richness of fatty dishes. Look for ginger that is heavy and hard; lightness in weight and wrinkled skin indicate that it's not very fresh. Its soft skin can be easily peeled with a metal spoon before using.

KAFFIR LIME LEAVES

Kaffir lime leaves lend a bright citrus aroma to many Thai dishes, including Thai Lemongrass and Prawn Soup (page 91) and Thai Red Curry Chicken and Green Bean Stir-Fry (page 113). The thick leaves are dark green and shiny on one side, and pale colored and porous on the back. They can be purchased fresh, frozen, or dried from Thai and Vietnamese markets, though the dried leaves are not as aromatic. Before adding to a soup or stir-fry, tear the leaves with your hands to release the flavors. Store unused kaffir lime leaves in a sealed bag in the freezer and they will keep for up to 3 months. If you're unable to find kaffir lime leaves, you can substitute bay leaves in some recipes as indicated.

LEMONGRASS

A type of grass grown and used widely in many tropical regions, lemongrass is common in Thai and Vietnamese cuisines. It lends a fragrant citrus aroma and flavor to soups, curries, stir-fries, and even tea. This zesty herb is sold by the stalk and pounded to release the most flavor (see How to Prepare Lemongrass, page 23).

LIMES

Limes are the most commonly used acidic ingredient in Thai cooking, and brighten up the flavors in salads, soups, and dips. Always add lime juice at the very end of cooking; heat can deteriorate its flavor.

NAPA CABBAGE

Napa cabbage is commonly used in stir-frying and braising in Chinese and Korean cooking, or as a dumpling or spring roll filling. It has yellowish white leaves and is more oblong than green cabbage. It can be stored in the crisper bin of the refrigerator for up to 2 weeks.

SCALLIONS

Also called green onions, scallions add a delicious onion-y flavor to stir-fries, soups, noodles, and rice dishes. Often, a recipe will specify white parts only, green parts only, or the entire scallion. The general rule is that you should use the white parts, which have a stronger flavor, at the beginning of cooking, whereas you should use the milder green parts toward the end of cooking or as a garnish (see more in How to Prepare Scallions, opposite).

SHIITAKE MUSHROOMS

Both fresh and dried mushrooms are commonly used in East and Southeast Asian cooking. They are extremely versatile and can be stir-fried, steamed, braised, grilled, or added to soups. Dishes that are Chinese or Chinese-influenced tend to favor dried shiitake mushrooms, which have a deep earthy aroma and contribute an umami flavor that is prized in Chinese cooking. The best dried shiitakes have thick caps with white fissures on top. Fresh shiitake are widely available in Western markets as well. Be sure to wipe the caps clean with a damp towel and remove the stems before using.

TATSOI

Also called spinach mustard or rosette bok choy, tatsoi has broad green leaves and a mild mustardy bite. Look for tatsoi with leaves that are dark and glossy green and avoid any bunches that are wilted, yellowing, or flowering. They can be eaten raw or lightly cooked, and are great in salads, stir-fries, or steamed dishes.

THAI BASIL

Native to Southeast Asia, Thai basil has a more robust, spicier flavor than its Italian counterpart. The purple color on the stem can also extend to the leaves. The peppery, anise-like flavor makes it an ideal component in noodle soups, summer rolls, salads, stir-fries, and curries.

SAUCES, PASTES, SYRUPS, AND FLAVORING OILS

CHINESE RICE WINE

Also known as Shaoxing cooking wine or yellow rice wine, this is an aged cooking wine that is yellowish in color and has a deep savory flavor. At Chinese grocery stores, look for the red-labeled Pagoda brand bottles; the bottles with yellow labels are sweetened. Dry sherry is a great substitute if you can't find Chinese rice wine. I don't recommend substituting mirin, a Japanese rice wine, because of its sweetness.

DOUBANJIANG (CHINESE FERMENTED CHILI BEAN PASTE)

This staple of Sichuan cuisine is a fermented paste made with fava beans or soybeans. It is produced in China and undergoes a long, strict fermentation process outdoors in earthenware jars, which makes it a bit impractical to feature as a homemade chili paste in this book. However, store-bought versions are easy to find in Chinese supermarkets.

HOW TO PREPARE LEMONGRASS

1. Hold the lemongrass by the yellow-green grass end. With the back edge of a chef's knife, pound the white part of the lemongrass to release the juices.

2. Thinly slice the white parts. Discard the yellow-green end.

HOW TO PREPARE SCALLIONS

Often, a recipe will specify white parts only, green parts only, or the entire scallion. The white parts, which have a stronger flavor, are used at the beginning of cooking, whereas the milder green parts are used toward the end of cooking or as a garnish. You can slice scallions straight across, or the traditional Chinese way of slicing them at an angle to expose more of the flavorful insides.

SHRIMP PASTE

TAMARIND PASTE

PALM SUGAR

MISO PASTE

SESAME OIL

DOUBANJIANG (CHINESE FERMENTED CHILI BEAN PASTE)

CHINESE RICE WINE

MIRIN

RICE VINEGAR

CHINESE BLACK VINEGAR

KECAP MANIS (INDONESIAN SWEET SOY SAUCE)

SOY SAUCE

OYSTER SAUCE

FISH SAUCE

HOISIN SAUCE

MIRIN

A pantry staple used in Japanese cooking, mirin is a rice wine with a lower alcohol and higher sugar content than sake. Its sweet flavor helps to balance out saltier sauces, like soy sauce or tamari. Mirin is extremely versatile and can be used in salad dressings, teriyaki sauces, marinades, and glazes for meat, fish, and vegetables. If you need a substitute for mirin, avoid using Chinese rice wine since it may be salted depending on the brand. Instead, opt for 1 tablespoon white wine or vermouth combined with ½ teaspoon sugar to replace 1 tablespoon mirin.

MISO

Miso is a thick fermented paste traditionally made from soybeans, salt, and a culture called *koji*, although newer varieties may use other grains. It's the base for fortifying the soup of the same name, and can also be used for glazes for meat, seafood, and vegetables. There are many types of miso, but the ones most widely available outside a Japanese market are red, yellow, and white. The darker the miso, the bolder the flavors tend to be. The recipes in this book call for white or yellow miso, which has a milder and slightly sweeter flavor than red miso.

FISH SAUCE

One of the backbones of Southeast Asian cuisines, fish sauce is made by fermenting fish, usually anchovies, and is extremely pungent. Use it sparingly; even a teaspoon or so will provide plenty of flavor. Well-refrigerated bottles will keep for at least one year.

HOISIN SAUCE

This sweetened soybean paste flavored with garlic and vinegar can be used as a marinade or sauce ingredient in Chinese cooking. A good brand to look for in Chinese markets is Koon Chun, which comes in a bottle with a yellow and purple-ish blue label.

OYSTER SAUCE

A staple of Cantonese and Chinese-Thai cooking, this dark, viscous sauce is made from oysters (or oyster extract), water, and salt. (Vegetarian oyster sauces use mushrooms for flavoring.) I recommend the brand Lee Kum Kee, which has been producing oyster sauce since the late 1800s.

BROWN RICE SYRUP

A sweetener derived from brown rice, rice syrup is a key ingredient in gochujang, both the traditional and simplified versions. If you can't find rice syrup, use honey or maple syrup as a substitute.

SESAME OIL

Used as either a cooking ingredient or condiment, sesame oil adds a lovely aroma to Chinese, Japanese, and Korean dishes. For the recipes in this book, use Asian sesame oils, which are toasted and dark amber in color, instead of light-colored Middle Eastern or Indian sesame oils from raw sesame seeds. Be sure to buy sesame oil that is sold in glass bottles; plastic makes the oil become rancid much more quickly.

SHRIMP PASTE

Shrimp paste is a funky-smelling, fermented paste made with finely crushed shrimp or krill mixed with salt. It is an essential ingredient in many Thai and Indonesian dishes. The flavor is intensely earthy and salty, and a little bit goes a long way.

SOY SAUCE AND DARK SOY SAUCE

Both types of soy sauce are dark, salty, and earthy, used both for seasoning food while cooking or at the table. Most of the recipes in this book call for regular soy sauce. Dark soy sauce, which is aged longer and has a richer color, is slightly sweeter and less salty, making it better for long cooking methods like roasting or braising. Whichever brand you choose, be sure that soybeans are one of the main ingredients; some brands use hydrolyzed vegetable protein to imitate a soy flavor.

Reduced-sodium soy sauce is a good substitute if it is made with soybeans and not artificial ingredients. Chinese soy sauces use little to no wheat in the brewing process. Japanese soy sauce, sometimes labeled "shoyu," is thinner and slightly sweeter than its Chinese counterpart, and tends to contain wheat. For Japanese soy sauces that do not contain wheat, see Tamari (below).

KECAP MANIS (INDONESIAN SWEET SOY SAUCE)

A staple in Indonesian cooking, kecap manis is a syrupy-thick soy sauce sweetened with palm sugar. It's a great ingredient for satays, marinades, stir-fries, soups, and glazes. ABC and Bango brand sweet soy sauces are widely popular and good to try. If you can't find kecap manis, substitute with 2 parts regular soy sauce and 1 part brown sugar.

TAMARI

In contrast to Japanese shoyu, tamari is a type of Japanese soy sauce that is traditionally made from the byproduct of miso production. It contains little or no wheat, and wheat-free tamari can be consumed by people with a gluten intolerance. Tamari has a darker color and bolder flavor than both Chinese soy sauce and shoyu, though it tends to also be less salty.

TAMARIND PASTE

Tamarind paste adds a prune-like sourness to Nam Prik Pao (page 82) and a variety of Thai and Indonesian dishes. Ready-to-use tamarind cooking paste, which just contains the fruit with the pod and seeds discarded, comes in a jar or plastic tub-like container. It is quite concentrated and will last a long time; store refrigerated after opening.

ON COOKING OILS

At home, I like to keep a variety of cooking oils on hand, most of which are versatile and suitable for high temperatures. The recipes in this book call for vegetable oil, but you can use other oils with high smoke points, including peanut, grapeseed, sunflower, safflower, canola, and certain brands of avocado oil. When in doubt, make sure the bottle lists the smoke point as 420°F or higher, or specifies that it's suitable for "high-heat cooking." I love using extra-virgin olive oil in the kitchen, but only in salad dressings and during times when I'm sautéing on very low heat, like toasting garlic. Also avoid using toasted sesame oil and coconut oil for high-heat cooking.

It's important to remember that the settings on your stove are relative, and some stoves are much more powerful than others. Even if you turn your stove to medium, the temperature of the oil in your pan continues to rise as you're cooking, and this is especially true with stir-fries and other dishes where there is little other liquid in the pan. My rule of thumb is any time I cook on medium heat or higher, I use a high-temperature cooking oil just to be safe.

VINEGARS

CHINESE BLACK VINEGAR

This aged dark vinegar made with glutinous rice has an earthy, tangy, and slightly sweet flavor. It is reminiscent of good balsamic vinegar, which can be used as a substitute. The best black vinegar to look for is Gold Plum brand Chinkiang vinegar, available at most Chinese markets.

RICE VINEGAR

This clear rice vinegar adds a bracing, acidic flavor to dishes. Chinese white rice vinegars tend to be sharper, while Japanese rice vinegars are a little mellower. Cider vinegar, which is slightly sweeter, can be used as a substitute. Don't use distilled malt vinegar as a substitute, as the flavor is much too abrasive.

SICHUAN PEPPERCORN

STAR ANISE

GROUND
TURMERIC

GROUND
CUMIN

WHOLE
CUMIN SEEDS

SPICES

CUMIN

Best known for its pervasiveness in Indian and Middle Eastern cooking, cumin is also frequently used in China and northern Thailand. You can buy cumin ground or as whole seeds. While preground cumin is more convenient to use, buying whole seeds and grinding before cooking will make a dish much more fragrant.

SICHUAN PEPPER/ SICHUAN PEPPERCORNS

Sichuan peppercorns may look like the red versions of black or white peppercorns, but they are actually tiny berries. Best known for their numbing properties and floral citrusy aroma, they bear no capsaicin, but are frequently paired with chilies in a number of Sichuan dishes. You can find Sichuan pepper whole or ground, but it is best to buy whole peppercorn and grind it yourself for the most flavor.

STAR ANISE

The Chinese often use whole or ground star anise to flavor cooking liquids for meat and poultry. It has a mild licorice flavor that pairs well with cinnamon, which it is often used alongside in braising liquids. Star anise is also one of the spices in Chinese five-spice powder.

TURMERIC

Ground turmeric is a golden yellow spice that comes from the root of a plant in the ginger family and has a pungent, earthy flavor with a slight gingery tinge. It is frequently used in Thai cooking, especially in curry pastes. When cooking with turmeric, be careful as the spice will leave a yellowish color on hands and clothing.

TOFU AND SOY-BASED PROTEINS

EDAMAME

Edamame are soybeans that have been harvested before fully maturing. The whole pods are most often served as a finger-food appetizers, though the beans can also be stir-fried or blanched and added to salads.

TEMPEH

Tempeh, fermented soybeans formed into a patty, has a dense texture and nutty, earthy flavor. The flavor may be off-putting to some people, so it is best when cooked with strong spices and sauces.

PRESSED TOFU

BAKED TOFU

TEMPEH

EDAMAME

TOFU

Tofu is a protein that is created by setting soy milk with a coagulant, similar to making cheese, and then forming the curds into a solid block. Pressed tofu comes in textures that range from soft to extra-firm, though I tend to prefer firm and extra-firm for soups and braises because they hold their shape better. For stir-fries and certain noodle dishes, I like to use smoked or baked tofu (which can be found in many natural groceries stores and even large chains such as Trader Joe's) for its firm, almost crisp texture on the outside and slightly softer texture on the inside.

RICE

WHITE RICE

Long-grain • Long-grain white rice is the type of rice most traditional to Southeast Asian and southern Chinese cooking, and it's my preferred type for the Thai, Indonesian, and Chinese dishes in this book. It's a little less starchy than short-grain rice, and the grains stay fluffy and separate after cooking, which makes it ideal for most types of rice preparations, especially fried rice. Jasmine rice, with its lightly floral aroma, is my favorite type of long-grain rice. (See Steamed White Rice, page 240.)

Short-grain • A staple of northern Chinese, Korean, and Japanese cooking, short-grain white rice tends to be starchier than its long-grain cousin. I tend to use this more for sushi and other preparations where stickiness is useful, but it's just as good for plain steamed rice to serve alongside other dishes. You could also use this for fried rice, but keep in mind it will be a little stickier.

BROWN RICE

Though not traditional to Asian cooking, brown rice can be used as a substitute for white rice in many of the recipes in this book. Look for long- or medium-grain brown rice, which is easier to cook than short-grain. It does take longer to prepare than white rice and has a shorter shelf life. (See Steamed Brown Rice, page 241.)

NOODLES

BEAN THREAD VERMICELLI NOODLES

These translucent threadlike noodles are made from mung beans and sold dry. They look almost identical to rice vermicelli noodles (see below), but are a little more opaque. Be sure to check that the ingredients list "mung beans" or "bean starch" as an ingredient instead of rice. Whereas rice vermicelli noodles are often stir-fried, bean thread noodles are used more often in soups and braises.

CHINESE WHEAT NOODLES

Chinese wheat noodles are usually made with a salted dough, so unlike Western pasta, they don't require the addition of salt in the water when they are boiled. Both dried and fresh noodles usually take less than 5 minutes to cook through.

RAMEN

There is such a wide variety of ramen noodles on the market that it is difficult to distinguish between the great and mediocre versions. If you can, find fresh ramen noodles, which tend to have a firmer bite than their dried counterparts. Sun Noodle is one of the best US-based makers and their products are worth seeking out.

RICE CAKES

Rice cakes, called *nian gao* in Mandarin Chinese and *tteok* in Korean, are made of steamed glutinous rice flour and other grains. Chinese rice cakes can be found in oval slices, whereas the Korean version also comes in a cylinder shape. With a chewy texture that acts as a sponge for soaking up flavors, both kinds are used in stews and stir-fries. I tend to prefer the oval slices since they cook much faster.

WIDE RICE NOODLES

Wide rice noodles, which range in width from ¼ inch to 1 inch, are used in noodle soups or stir-fries. Fresh wide rice noodles used to be difficult to find outside of Asian markets but are becoming more widely available at stores such as Whole Foods.

RICE VERMICELLI NOODLES

Sometimes called rice stick noodles, rice vermicelli noodles are made with rice flour, white in color, and about the diameter of angel hair pasta. They are often used for stir-fries, soups, or the fillings of spring rolls. They look almost identical to bean thread vermicelli noodles (see above), so check that the package lists rice as the main ingredient.

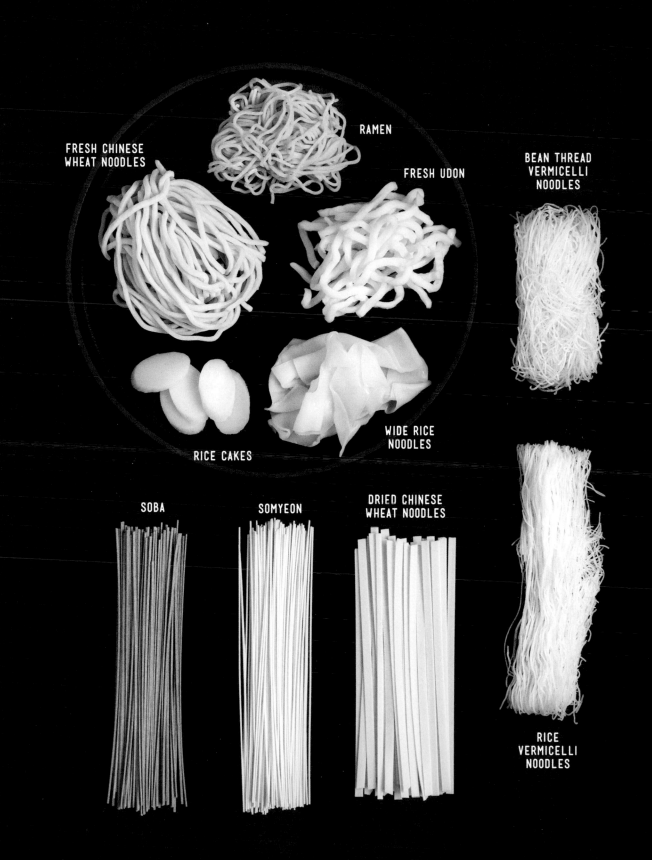

RAMEN

FRESH CHINESE
WHEAT NOODLES

FRESH UDON

BEAN THREAD
VERMICELLI
NOODLES

RICE CAKES

WIDE RICE
NOODLES

SOBA

SOMYEON

DRIED CHINESE
WHEAT NOODLES

RICE
VERMICELLI
NOODLES

SOBA

Made with buckwheat flour, soba noodles have a strong nutty flavor and range in color from light gray to darkish brown. They are wonderful to add to soups or chilled noodle salads. Whether you use fresh or dried soba noodles, seek out ones that are on the thicker side; they tend to hold up better during cooking.

SOMYEON

These thin Korean wheat noodles have roughly the thickness of angel hair pasta. You can use them for both hot dishes and cold dishes like Korean Chilled Spicy Noodles (Bibim Guksu), page 189. If you can't find *somyeon*, you can substitute very thin Chinese wheat noodles.

UDON

Udon noodles are wheat noodles with a thick, chewy texture. They are most often used in noodle soups, though you can also pan-fry them with meat and vegetables. I recommend using fresh udon noodles whenever possible, since the dried version doesn't plump up to the same thick texture when cooked.

OTHER DRIED PRODUCTS

BARLEY MALT POWDER

A key ingredient in making traditional gochujang, barley malt powder is barley that has been fermented, then dried and ground. You can find it in Korean grocery stores under the name *yeotgireum garu* or health food stores or online.

DRIED SCALLOPS

Also known as *conpoy*, dried scallops are prized in Chinese cooking for their rich umami flavor. They are made from the adductor muscles of scallops and range in price from $20 to $100 a pound, depending on size. (The priciest large ones are used as gifts for weddings and other special events.) I stick to the more economical smaller scallops, which lend a delicious briny flavor to XO sauce. Dried scallops can be stored in an airtight container in the refrigerator for up to a year.

DRIED SHRIMP

Dried shrimp add a briny earthiness to broth, stir-fries, and dim sum dishes. It is also one of the key components in XO sauce. Choose the kind that are larger and reddish orange, and avoid the tinier white opaque kind with visible black eyes, which are much blander in comparison. Stored in an airtight jar in the fridge, they can last for up to a year.

FERMENTED BLACK BEANS

Also called Chinese dried black beans, fermented black beans are actually not the same kind of black beans you get in Latin American food, but rather black soybeans that have been fermented and salted. They add an incredibly funky depth to Chinese dishes. Usually sold in plastic packages, they should be transferred to an airtight glass storage container immediately after opening and stored in the back of the fridge, where they will keep for up to a year. Right before using, rinse the beans under cold water to rehydrate them and mash them with the back of a spoon to release more flavor.

NORI

Nori, a type of seaweed, is typically sold in packs of roasted, unseasoned sheets for sushi-making. They are also great for cutting into strips to use as toppings for ramen bowls. For the ramen recipes, in a pinch you can use the small sheets that come in snack packs, but be aware that these are salted and a bit oily, unlike nori sheets for sushi-making.

PALM SUGAR

Palm sugar is made by boiling down the sap of various palm trees, including the sugar palm, coconut palm, and palmyra palm. It has a wonderful maple-like sweetness and helps to balance out the spiciness of chilies, the saltiness of soy or fish sauce, and the acidity of vinegars and citruses in Southeast Asian cooking. In a pinch, you can use brown sugar or maple sugar as a substitute. Dark brown sugar has a closer texture to that of palm sugar, but is sweeter and stronger in molasses flavor, so I tend to prefer light brown sugar as a substitute.

SESAME SEEDS (WHITE OR BLACK)

These tiny seeds are often used in Chinese, Japanese, and Korean cooking to add a nutty aroma to the finished dish. White sesame seeds are raw and can be used as is or lightly toasted, while black sesame seeds have a much deeper flavor. Like most nuts and seeds, sesame seeds are prone to rancidity, so storing them in the freezer or refrigerator keeps them fresh. Lightly toasting them in a dry skillet brings out their flavor.

RICE FLOUR

Sometime labeled "rice powder" in Asian grocery stores, rice flour is used to make the rice noodles eaten in Southeast Asia and Southern China. It is also a great binder and adds a light texture to dishes such as Indonesian Corn Fritters (Bakwan Jagung) on page 45 and Thai Omelet (Khao Jiao) on page 89. Be sure to purchase packages labeled "rice flour" rather than "sweet rice flour," which is made from glutinous rice and is much starchier (page 36).

BAMBOO STEAMER

MORTAR AND
PESTLE

SWEET RICE FLOUR (GLUTINOUS RICE FLOUR)

Sweet rice flour is ground from short-grain glutinous rice, also known as "sticky rice." It is much starchier and stickier than regular rice flour, and is one of the key ingredients in making traditional gochujang. It is also sometimes labeled "mochiko flour" in Asian grocery stores.

WAKAME

Wakame is a dried seaweed most often used in miso soup and seaweed salads. It has a mild flavor and soft texture. Simply rehydrate it for 10 to 15 minutes and it's ready to be eaten raw or lightly cooked.

EQUIPMENT

BAMBOO STEAMER

Bamboo steamers are often sold in three-piece sets, with two trays and one lid. They range in size from 6 inches in diameter to around 2 feet, and are fantastic for steaming a variety of Chinese dishes, including dumplings, vegetables, and fish.

DOLSOT

A small stone pot used for both cooking and serving, a *dolsot* is used for various rice preparations in Korean cuisine, including bibimbap. Because the dolsot retains its heat after being removed from the stove, the rice continues to cook and forms a nice crust on the bottom. Bibimbap can also be made in a pot and transferred to a bowl after cooking, though it won't have the scorched rice layer that many crave in a traditional bibimbap.

FOOD PROCESSOR

A small food processor is handy to own if you plan on making chili sauces regularly. Depending on the size, it can produce hot sauces in volume. Basic models cost about $20 and take up little room in your cabinet.

MICROPLANE GRATER

A Microplane grater is an ideal tool for extracting lime or lemon zest or grating ginger for extracting ginger juice. In the absence of a Microplane grater, you can use the finest holes on a cheese grater instead.

MORTAR AND PESTLE

A mortar and pestle can be used to crush whole spices, mash garlic, and pound chili pastes. An electric spice grinder or food processor may do the job more quickly, but a mortar and pestle can generally coax more flavors out of the ingredient and give you more control over the texture. Whether you use a stone, marble, or wooden version, be sure the bowl holds at least 2 cups if you plan on using it to make chili pastes.

DEEP-FRY THERMOMETER

A deep-fry thermometer, also called a candy thermometer, is essential for accurate deep-frying. It will allow you to know precisely when the oil is hot enough, thus preventing the food from absorbing too much oil when added too early or quickly burning when added too late.

ONGGI

An *onggi* is a Korean earthenware crock used for fermenting kimchi, wines, gochujang, and other sauces. They range in sizes from small tabletop versions (also called *hangari*) to larger ones a few feet high that are meant to be stored outdoors. To clean an onggi, use only warm or hot water and scrub well; soap particles can become lodged in the porous walls and transfer to your food.

TONGS

A pair of well-made, sturdy tongs are handy for tossing noodles, flipping meats and vegetables when roasting, and transferring food when deep-frying.

WOK

If you are looking to do a fair amount of Chinese cooking or stir-frying, you may want to invest in a wok. The large bowl shape allows you to toss and stir more vigorously than in a skillet without food flying out, and retains heat better during the cooking process. The best woks are made of carbon steel or cast iron, and must be seasoned before using. A well-made wok will cost only $20 to $30 and should last a lifetime with proper care.

WOK SPATULA

Wok cooking can be done with regular spatulas and metal or wooden spoons, but a wok spatula is a versatile tool to have in the kitchen. This wide, shovel-shaped spatula has rounded edges that match the curves inside a wok and allow you to toss and scoop up food and sauces easily. Most wok spatulas are made of stainless steel, which allow them to withstand high temperatures and frequent use.

ONGGI

DOLSOT

SAMBAL OELEK

SAMBAL OELEK

MAKES ABOUT 2 CUPS Sambals are chili sauces or pastes native to Indonesia and Malaysia, more beloved and central to national identity than even ketchup is to Americans. Sambals are so versatile that they are used with everything, including noodles, rice, raw vegetables, soups, grilled fish, fried chicken, and even breakfast eggs. In Indonesia alone there are thousands of varieties of sambal, which vary depending on the type of chilies used, other ingredients, texture, and region in which they are made. There are sambals that highlight coconut, lemongrass, mango, pineapple, tomato, tamarind, peanut, mackerel, shrimp paste, Sichuan pepper, strawberries, or even fermented durian.

While many sambals include fried, roasted, smoked, or fermented ingredients, we'll focus on sambal oelek, a basic sambal using raw ingredients. It's extremely versatile and can be used as the base for making other sambals, or as a go-to chili sauce for cuisines outside of Indonesian and Malaysian. The bright red sauce studded with chili seeds, with a lightly chunky texture similar to that of a coarse relish, is a wonderful springboard to the world of complex and nuanced chili sauces.

Sambal oelek is traditionally ground with a mortar and pestle (*oelek* means "ground by stone mortar" in Indonesian), but you can easily make it in a food processor. Feel free to experiment with the types of fresh chilies; choose jalapeños or Fresnos for a medium-hot sambal, serranos for a very hot one, and cayennes if you'd prefer your sambal fiery and tear-inducing.

1 pound fresh red chilies 2 to 4 inches long (preferably cayenne, serrano, jalapeño, or Fresno), stemmed and cut into large pieces (for easier processing)

4 cloves garlic, peeled

1/4 cup fresh lime juice (2 to 3 limes)

2 tablespoons distilled white vinegar

2 tablespoons palm sugar or brown sugar

4 teaspoons salt

In a food processor, combine all the ingredients and pulse for 2 to 3 minutes to form a fairly smooth sauce (if it still seems chunky after 3 minutes, pulse for 1 to 2 minutes longer). Store in a container with a tight-fitting lid. The sambal will keep in the fridge for up to 3 months or in the freezer for up to 6 months.

BALINESE GRILLED SHRIMP SKEWERS

SERVES 4 AS PART OF A MULTICOURSE MEAL Grilled shrimp can be fantastic with just a dash of salt and pepper, but these fiery shrimp skewers are guaranteed to be a crowd-pleaser at summer cookouts. The sambal oelek gets mixed with more aromatic lemongrass and garlic, along with turmeric, coriander, and some palm sugar to balance out the heat. The skewers need only an hour or so of marinating before grilling. The shrimp are medium-spicy off the grill, but if you'd like to bump it up to very spicy, serve it with extra sambal on the side.

1/4 cup sambal oelek, plus more for serving

1 stalk lemongrass, lower part pounded and thinly sliced

2 cloves garlic, peeled

1 tablespoon palm sugar or light brown sugar

1/2 teaspoon ground turmeric

1/2 teaspoon ground coriander

1 teaspoon salt

24 jumbo shrimp (about 1 1/2 pounds), peeled and deveined

Vegetable oil, for the grill

SPECIAL EQUIPMENT
8 bamboo skewers

1. In a food processor, combine the sambal, lemongrass, garlic, palm sugar, turmeric, coriander, and salt. Blend until a smooth paste forms.

2. In a large bowl, toss the shrimp with the marinade. Cover and refrigerate for 1 hour.

3. Meanwhile, soak the bamboo skewers in water for at least 15 minutes to prevent them from burning on the grill.

4. Preheat a grill to medium-high. Thread 3 shrimp on each of the 8 skewers. Brush the grill grates with some oil. Grill the shrimp until pink on the outside and firm inside, 2 to 3 minutes per side. Transfer the cooked skewers to a platter and serve with extra sambal oelek on the side.

INDONESIAN CORN FRITTERS (BAKWAN JAGUNG)

SERVES 4 TO 6 AS AN APPETIZER OR SNACK In Indonesia, corn fritters known as *bakwan jagung* are a beloved street snack that is served from morning to night. They are also easy to whip up at home. If you're in the height of corn season, fresh ears of corn are best to use for this recipe, but you can always substitute canned corn. The fritters come out light, crispy, and perfectly matched for the sambal, tamarind, and lime dipping sauce. Leftover batter will keep in the fridge for up to 2 days.

SAUCE

- 1/4 cup sambal oelek
- 2 tablespoons tamarind paste
- 1 tablespoon fish sauce or soy sauce
- 1 tablespoon fresh lime juice
- 1 tablespoon palm sugar or brown sugar

FRITTERS

- 1 cup rice flour
- 2 large eggs, beaten
- 2 teaspoons salt
- 1/4 teaspoon freshly ground black pepper
- 2 ears corn, kernels cut from the cob, or 1 1/2 cups canned corn, drained
- 1 large shallot, finely chopped
- 2 scallions, finely chopped
- 4 cloves garlic, minced
- 2 cups canola, peanut, or vegetable oil

1. Prepare the sauce: In a small bowl, whisk together the sambal, tamarind paste, fish sauce, lime juice, and palm sugar. Set aside.

2. Prepare the fritters: In a large bowl, whisk together the rice flour, eggs, salt, and pepper until a thick batter forms. Stir in the corn, shallot, scallions, and garlic.

3. In a cast-iron pan or other heavy-bottomed pan with sides at least 2 inches high, heat the oil until the temperature reads 325°F on a deep-fry thermometer. Working in batches, scoop 1 heaping spoonful of mixture per fritter into the pan. Fry until golden brown all over, about 2 minutes on each side. Place on a plate lined with paper towels to drain. Serve warm with the tamarind-chili sauce.

SPICY PEANUT AND GINGER CUCUMBER CUPS

SERVES 4 AS AN APPETIZER OR SNACK A few years ago I catered a birthday dinner where many of the appetizers had to be vegan and work as finger foods. Looking for ideas that weren't run-of-the-mill, I decided to make a peanut butter spread with sambal and ginger and serve it in cucumber cups. They work as pretty filling appetizers that are spicy yet refreshing at the same time! Small measuring spoons work best for hollowing out the cucumbers.

2 large cucumbers or
   4 to 5 Kirby cucumbers,
   washed and unpeeled
1/2 cup smooth peanut butter
3 tablespoons sambal oelek

1 teaspoon rice vinegar
1/2 teaspoon sea salt
1 teaspoon minced
   fresh ginger

1 large carrot, grated
2 scallions, finely chopped
1/4 cup peanuts, chopped

1. Trim the ends from the cucumbers and cut crosswise into slices about 1 inch thick. Using a small measuring spoon, scoop out about 1/2 teaspoon of the inside from each slice. Arrange the cucumbers on plates for easy filling.

2. In a large bowl, mix together the peanut butter, sambal, rice vinegar, sea salt, and ginger until smooth. Stir in the carrot and scallions. Spoon 1 to 2 teaspoons filling into each cucumber cup, with enough on top to form a dome (using two spoons will make the filling easier). Garnish the top of each cup with chopped peanuts and serve.

INDONESIAN FRIED RICE (NASI GORENG)

SERVES 4 AS PART OF A MULTICOURSE MEAL *Nasi goreng*, or Indonesian fried rice, has been called the national dish of Indonesia. Not surprisingly, there are many variations, but the truest versions have three key ingredients—sambal for spice, shrimp paste for funky depth, and kecap manis (Indonesian sweet soy sauce) for the caramelized sweet and salty flavors. This is a basic version, but feel free to add chicken, shrimp, beef, or other proteins. It is stronger, smokier, and earthier than other fried rice dishes around Asia and one that you'll want to make again and again.

4 cups cooked white or brown rice, refrigerated overnight

3 tablespoons sambal oelek

3 tablespoons kecap manis (sweet soy sauce)

1 tablespoon shrimp paste

5 tablespoons vegetable oil

2 shallots, finely chopped

2 cloves garlic, minced

2 fresh bird's eye chilies or Thai spur chilies, thinly sliced

4 large eggs

1/4 teaspoon salt

2 Kirby cucumbers, cut into slices 1/4 inch thick

2 medium tomatoes, sliced

2 scallions, thinly sliced, for garnish

1. Break up the cold cooked rice into smaller clumps.

2. In a small bowl, whisk together the sambal, kecap manis, and shrimp paste. Set aside.

3. Heat a wok or large skillet over medium-high heat until a bead of water sizzles and evaporates on contact. Add 3 tablespoons of the vegetable oil and swirl to coat the bottom. Add the rice and break up any remaining clumps with a spatula. Stir-fry until the rice starts to turn golden, 2 to 3 minutes. Add the shallots, garlic, and chilies and cook for another 30 to 60 seconds. Add the sambal mixture and stir to mix evenly. Cover to keep warm while you cook the eggs.

4. In another large skillet, heat the remaining 2 tablespoons oil. Fry the eggs sunny-side-up until the whites are set. Sprinkle the salt over the eggs.

5. Divide the rice onto individual plates and top each plate with an egg. Add the cucumbers and tomatoes to the side. Top with scallions and serve.

TEMPEH AND GREEN BEANS IN SAMBAL

SERVES 4 AS PART OF A MULTICOURSE MEAL, OR 2 AS A FULL MEAL Tempeh is a nutty-tasting soy protein that originated in Indonesia, so it's no surprise the country's cuisine boasts many tasty ways to cook with it. One of my favorites is this stir-fry with tempeh and green beans in a sambal sauce mixed with sweet soy sauce, turmeric, shallots, and garlic. You'll need to crumble the tempeh with your hands before adding to the wok or skillet, but after that, the cooking part is incredibly quick.

8 ounces tempeh or
   extra-firm tofu

1/4 cup sambal oelek

2 tablespoons kecap manis
   (sweet soy sauce)

1/2 teaspoon ground turmeric

2 tablespoons vegetable oil

2 shallots, chopped

3 cloves garlic, minced

1 pound green beans,
   trimmed and cut into 2-inch
   lengths

1/2 cup water

1 lime, cut into wedges

1 handful unsalted dry-
   roasted peanuts, chopped

1. In a medium bowl, crumble the tempeh with your hands and set aside.

2. In a small bowl, whisk together the sambal, kecap manis, and turmeric. Set aside.

3. In a wok or large skillet, heat the vegetable oil over medium-high heat. Add the tempeh and stir-fry until golden, 2 to 3 minutes. Add the shallots, garlic, and green beans and stir-fry for another minute. Add the water, cover, and cook until the green beans are crisp-tender, 3 to 4 minutes.

4. Uncover and stir in the sambal mixture. Transfer to a serving dish with limes on the side, top with the peanuts, and serve.

INDONESIAN SPICY FRUIT SALAD (SAMBAL ROJAK)

SERVES 4 AS A DESSERT *Rojak* is a spicy, tangy, and sweet fruit salad found in Indonesia, Malaysia, and Singapore. While the Malay and Singaporean versions often include crackers and tofu, Indonesian rojak is a much simpler affair, usually consisting of just fresh fruits and vegetables. For my minimalist version, I toss together pineapples, mangoes, and lychees, but you can really use any combination of fruits such as melons, apples, pears, grapes, strawberries, guavas, dragon fruit, or starfruit. The sambal and tamarind sauce add a touch of spiciness, but the salad should be more refreshing than fiery.

8 ounces cut pineapple

2 mangoes, peeled and cut into bite-size cubes

1 pound fresh lychees, peeled and pitted, or one 15- to 20-ounce can lychees, drained

3 tablespoons sambal oelek

2 tablespoons palm sugar or light brown sugar

1 tablespoon tamarind paste

1/4 teaspoon salt

1/4 cup unsalted roasted peanuts, finely chopped

1. In a large bowl, combine the pineapple, mangoes, and lychees.

2. In a small bowl, whisk together the sambal, palm sugar, tamarind paste, 2 tablespoons water, and the salt. Add the sambal dressing to the large bowl, toss with the fruit, and transfer to a serving dish. Top with the peanuts and serve.

HURTS SO GOOD

It may be counterintuitive for humans to crave food that causes our eyes to water, tongues to burn, and bodies to sweat. So why do we come back to chili sauces and spicy food again and again? As it turns out, we get a sort of "runner's high" from spicy food. When you bite into a cayenne pepper or taste a fiery Thai curry, the capsaicin from the chilies hits your tongue and the pain receptors in your mouth. In response, your body releases dopamine and endorphins to cope with the pain, which heightens your senses and leads to the type of buzz or euphoria you get from other things such as exercise, roller coasters, love, or drugs. But don't worry; capsaicin isn't known to have addictive properties, so it's safe to keep drizzling or even dousing your food with Sriracha.

INDONESIAN LEMONGRASS AND SAMBAL BEEF STEW

SERVES 4 AS PART OF A MULTICOURSE MEAL This glorious beef stew is one of those dishes that will perfume your entire home while it simmers on the stove. The beef simmers for about an hour with lemongrass, sambal, chilies, coconut milk, and spices, while kaffir lime leaves are tossed in at the end. Be sure to choose beef shank, beef chuck, or another well-marbled cut and cook at a bare simmer so the meat becomes meltingly tender. And you'll want to have plenty of rice on hand to sop up the rich, spicy sauce.

2 stalks lemongrass, lower part pounded and thinly sliced (see How to Prepare Lemongrass, page 23)

3 shallots, peeled

6 cloves garlic, peeled

3 fresh chilies, such as bird's eye, Thai spur, or serrano

1/2 tablespoon chopped fresh galangal

1/2 tablespoon chopped fresh ginger

1/2 teaspoon ground coriander

1/2 teaspoon ground turmeric

6 tablespoons vegetable oil, plus more as needed

2 pounds beef shank or beef chuck, cut into 1-inch cubes

One 13.5-ounce can full-fat coconut milk

1/3 cup sambal oelek

3 tablespoons kecap manis (sweet soy sauce), or 2 tablespoons regular soy sauce plus 1 tablespoon brown sugar

3 kaffir lime leaves, roughly torn

Salt

1. In a food processor, combine the lemongrass, shallots, garlic, chilies, galangal, ginger, coriander, turmeric, and 3 tablespoons of the vegetable oil. Pulse until a smooth paste forms (if the mixture is still too rough, add 2 more tablespoons of vegetable oil).

2. In a large bowl, combine the beef cubes with the lemongrass paste and mix thoroughly. Let sit at room temperature for 10 minutes.

3. Heat a wok, Dutch oven, or large skillet over medium-high heat. Add the remaining 3 tablespoons vegetable oil and swirl to coat the bottom. Add the beef to the pan and sear until golden brown on the outside, about 2 minutes. Add the coconut milk, sambal, kecap manis, and kaffir lime leaves and bring the mixture to a boil. Reduce the heat to a bare simmer and cook until the beef is tender and cooked through, for 1 hour to 1 hour 10 minutes. Adjust the seasoning with salt if necessary. Transfer the beef to a serving dish and serve.

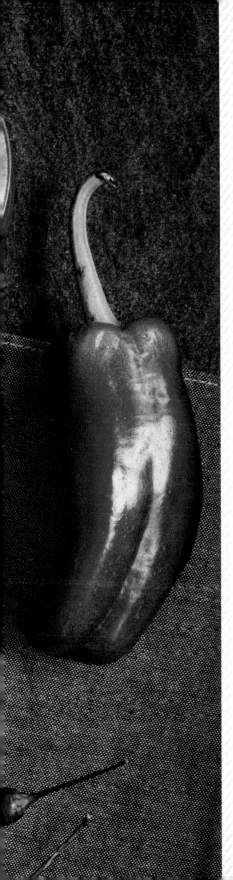

SRIRACHA

FRESH SRIRACHA

MAKES 1 TO 1½ CUPS Most readers may know of Sriracha as a sauce that comes in a bottle with a rooster on the label, but the traditional version from Thailand has a deeper, more balanced flavor. Originally produced in the seaside town of Sri Racha (see Sriracha—A Short History on the facing page), the piquant bright red sauce is a simple combination of fresh red chilies, garlic, vinegar, sugar, and salt.

While there are both fresh and fermented versions of Sriracha, I prefer the lighter flavor of fresh Sriracha, which tastes closer to the original Thai versions and is much easier to make. In Thailand, Holland chilies are commonly used to make Sriracha, but are difficult to find here; instead, fully ripened red jalapeños are the best comparable substitute. If you'd prefer a slightly fruitier and smokier flavor, you can also try Fresno chilies. I love using palm sugar for a bit of rounded sweetness, or you can use brown sugar for a deeper hit of molasses; the sugar helps to balance out the heat in the Sriracha and neither type is too cloying.

Simmering the sauce for about 5 minutes will break down the chili peppers and soften them to create the smooth consistency. Be sure to have a wire-mesh sieve or strainer on hand for straining, to achieve the signature smooth texture. Using jalapeños or Fresno chilies will yield a Sriracha with spiciness on par with store-bought bottles, but feel free to mix in some bird's eye chilies, Thai spur chilies, cayennes, or serranos for a spicier blend.

1 pound fresh red jalapeño or Fresno chilies, finely chopped

6 cloves garlic, smashed

⅓ cup rice vinegar

3 tablespoons palm sugar or brown sugar

2 teaspoons kosher salt

1. In a small saucepan, combine the chilies, garlic, rice vinegar, sugar, salt, and ⅔ cup water. Bring the mixture to a simmer over medium-high heat and cook for about 5 minutes, until the liquid is slightly reduced. Set aside to cool to room temperature.

2. Transfer the mixture to a food processor and puree until a very smooth liquid forms (the seeds will still be intact), about 5 minutes. Pour the mixture into a fine-mesh sieve set over a bowl, pressing on the solids with a spoon or spatula to extract as much sauce as possible. The Sriracha can be transferred to a jar and refrigerated for up to 1 month.

SRIRACHA—A SHORT HISTORY

The story of the original Sriracha dates back to the 1930s to a woman named Thanom Chakkapok, who lived in Sri Racha, Thailand, a sleepy beachside town about seventy miles south of Bangkok. She had created a sauce she called Sriraja Panich to give to friends and family, and they encouraged her to sell the sauce commercially. (Si Racha, Sriracha, and Sriraja are all Roman phonetic approximations of the same name.) Sriraja Panich became incredibly successful around Thailand, so much so that many Thai companies started producing their own versions of Sriracha. Now it's owned and sold by Thai Theparos Food Products, a large packaged food company in Thailand.

Tangy, runny, with hints of garlic, Thai Sriracha certainly had an influence on David Tran, a Vietnamese immigrant of Chinese ancestry who came to the US in the 1970s as a refugee. While still in Vietnam, he and his family had grown chilies and made hot sauces for a living, and after moving to California, he started selling a satay sauce, sambal oelek, chili garlic sauce, and finally, a Sriracha sauce. He named the company Huy Fong, after the boat that brought him to the US, and used the rooster as a logo, after his birth year on the Chinese zodiac calendar.

Made with vibrant red jalapeños, Sriracha came in a plastic squeeze bottle and was thicker, spicier, and less tangy than the Thai original. Because of Sriracha's versatility and convenience, the company went from a family operation in a small LA Chinatown storefront to currently selling over $80 million in products every year. It also seems to be a gateway hot sauce for Americans dipping their toes into spicy Asian food. While the rooster brand is what immediately comes to mind when you think of Sriracha, it's worth trying out the original Sriraja Panich for its more nuanced flavors, or better yet, make your own homemade version with no preservatives and the room to tweak the spice and texture to your liking.

SRIRACHA WHOLE-KERNEL CORNBREAD

MAKES 16 SQUARES In the summer and early fall, it's peak season for sweet corn and chili peppers at farmers' markets. So I love using homemade Sriracha in buttermilk cornbread. Whole kernels not only add a wonderful texture to the cornbread but also keep it from drying out when cooled to room temperature. Mildly spicy is what I prefer for baked goods, but if you prefer spicier, you can add some minced jalapeño to the batter.

1 stick (4 ounces) unsalted butter, melted, plus more for greasing the pan

1/2 cup sugar

2 tablespoons honey

2 large eggs

1 cup buttermilk

1 cup all-purpose flour

1 cup finely ground cornmeal

1/2 teaspoon baking soda

1/2 teaspoon salt

2 ears corn, kernels cut from the cob, or 1 1/2 cups canned corn, drained

1 fresh jalapeño, minced, optional

4 tablespoons Sriracha

1. Preheat the oven to 375°F. Grease a 9 x 9-inch baking pan with butter.

2. In a large bowl, combine the melted butter, sugar, and honey. Whisk in the eggs one at a time until well incorporated and smooth. Add the buttermilk and stir until smooth.

3. In another large bowl, sift together the flour, cornmeal, baking soda, and salt. Add the flour mixture to the wet ingredients 1/3 to 1/2 cup at a time, mixing well after each addition, until there are few or no lumps. Stir in the corn, jalapeño, and 2 tablespoons of the Sriracha. Pour the batter into the prepared pan. With a squeeze bottle or spoon, drizzle the remaining 2 tablespoons Sriracha in three parallel lines over the batter. Use a butter knife to create a marbled pattern by running it through the top of the batter at right angles to the lines.

4. Bake the cornbread until a toothpick inserted in the middle comes out clean, 40 to 45 minutes. Check at 20 or 25 minutes and if the top begins to brown too much around, cover the top with foil.

5. Remove from the oven and cool for 10 minutes before cutting into the cornbread. This will keep for 3 to 4 days at room temperature or up to 1 week in the fridge.

SRIRACHA HUMMUS WITH SUN-DRIED TOMATOES AND TOASTED GARLIC

SERVES 4 This is a spicier, smokier take on traditional hummus, but not so spicy that it scorches your tongue and throat. The sun-dried tomatoes add a lovely tanginess and the toasted garlic makes the hummus extra aromatic. And of course the recipe scales up for larger quantities, so it's an easy appetizer to whip up for all those summer barbecues, picnics, and other parties. Serve with chips, pita bread, or your favorite raw vegetables.

One 16-ounce can chickpeas (garbanzo beans), drained

3/4 cup plus 1 tablespoon extra-virgin olive oil

3 tablespoons Sriracha

2 tablespoons tahini

2 tablespoons fresh lemon juice

2 tablespoons minced garlic (about 2 cloves)

1 teaspoon salt, or to taste

1/4 cup sun-dried tomatoes, chopped

1/2 teaspoon crushed red chili flakes

1. In a food processor or blender, combine the chickpeas, 3/4 cup of the olive oil, the Sriracha, tahini, lemon juice, 1 tablespoon of the garlic, and the salt. Puree until smooth. Adjust the seasoning with more salt if you'd like. Transfer the hummus to a bowl.

2. In a small skillet, heat the remaining 1 tablespoon olive oil over low heat. Add the remaining 1 tablespoon garlic and cook just until golden and toasted, being careful to not let the garlic burn, about 30 seconds. Transfer the garlic and garlic oil to a bowl and mix with the sun-dried tomatoes and chili flakes.

3. Drizzle the garlic-chili mixture over the hummus and serve.

SRIRACHA LIME GARLIC WINGS

SERVES 4 The key to making these spicy, juicy, and zesty wings is a long marinating time (at least 3 hours, or overnight) for the flavors to seep into the chicken. I like to use 1/2 cup Sriracha in the marinade for moderately spicy wings, but you can double the amount for more fiery wings. Before you're ready for dinner, just pop the wings into the oven for about 30 minutes. These are the perfect spicy appetizer for your next game night or cookout.

2 pounds chicken wings, tips removed, wingettes and drumettes separated

8 cloves garlic, minced

1/2 cup Sriracha

1/4 cup tomato paste

3 tablespoons tamarind paste

1/4 cup soy sauce

3 tablespoons fresh lime juice (about 2 limes)

2 tablespoons honey

2 tablespoons sesame oil

1 teaspoon toasted sesame seeds

3 tablespoons grated lime zest (from about 2 limes)

1. To marinate the chicken wings, in a large bowl, combine the garlic, Sriracha, tomato paste, tamarind paste, soy sauce, lime juice, honey, and sesame oil. Place the wingettes and drumettes in a gallon freezer bag and pour the marinade over the chicken. Seal and shake the bag so the wings are coated with marinade. Let sit for at least 3 hours, or overnight.

2. Preheat the oven to 375°F. Line baking sheets with foil or parchment paper.

3. Place the wings on the baking sheets and bake until the wings are golden brown, 25 to 30 minutes. Transfer to a plate, sprinkle with the sesame seeds and lime zest, and serve.

SRIRACHA SHAKSHUKA

SERVES 4 TO 6 *Shakshuka,* a beautiful mess of simmered tomatoes and eggs that is a staple of Middle Eastern cuisines, traditionally employs fresh chilies, cayenne, or harissa for heat. My go-to brunch version, however, combines homemade Sriracha with cumin and smoked paprika for flavor, for those lazy Sunday mornings when cutting up fresh chilies is one step too many. Be sure to serve this with plenty of pita, challah, or other favorite bread to sop up the sauce.

2 tablespoons vegetable oil

3 cloves garlic, minced

1 large onion, diced

1 bell pepper, diced

One 14.5-ounce can whole peeled plum tomatoes

4 tablespoons Sriracha

2 teaspoons ground cumin

2 teaspoons smoked paprika

1 teaspoon salt

¼ teaspoon freshly ground black pepper

4 to 6 large eggs

1 cup pitted olives, sliced

Chopped parsley, for garnish

1. In an 8- to 10-inch skillet, heat the vegetable oil over medium heat. Add the garlic and onion and gently sauté until the onions are translucent, about 2 minutes. Add the bell pepper and cook for another minute. Slowly stir in the tomatoes with the can juices, and carefully break up the tomatoes with a spatula. Stir in 3 tablespoons of the Sriracha, the cumin, smoked paprika, salt, and black pepper. Allow the mixture to simmer for 15 to 20 minutes to thicken slightly. Adjust the seasoning with more salt and pepper if needed.

2. Crack the eggs one at a time into the tomato mixture, spacing them out evenly. Spoon a little of the tomato sauce over the edges of the egg whites, but leave the egg yolks exposed. Reduce the heat to medium. Cover and simmer until the whites are cooked through but the yolks are still a little bit runny, 5 to 8 minutes.

3. Remove from the heat and sprinkle the olives on top. Drizzle the remaining 1 tablespoon Sriracha over the eggs. Garnish with parsley and serve in the pan.

SHANGHAI HOT SAUCE NOODLES

SERVES 2 When I lived in Shanghai, *la jiang mian* was found on almost every street corner, at quick eats restaurants that catered to bustling lunch crowds. A piping hot bowl of noodles and spicy broth with tofu, peanuts, and a generous helping of chili sauce was the ideal quick lunch, and I slurped countless bowls a week. In Shanghai, the restaurants usually only use *doubanjiang* (a Chinese fermented, salted chili bean paste; see page 22) for the heat. At home, however, I like to pair doubanjiang with Sriracha to make a version that retains the same heat but is less salty than the restaurant versions.

5 tablespoons vegetable oil

½ cup raw peanuts

2 tablespoons doubanjiang (Chinese chili bean paste)

2 tablespoons Sriracha

1 small onion, finely diced

1 large carrot, finely diced

8 ounces smoked or baked tofu, cut into ½-inch cubes

1 teaspoon grated fresh ginger

2 teaspoons sugar

5 cups vegetable broth

1 pound fresh Chinese noodles, or 8 ounces dried noodles

2 scallions, finely chopped

1. Heat a wok or large pan over medium-high heat until a drop of water sizzles and evaporates on contact. Add 3 tablespoons of the vegetable oil. Add the peanuts and fry until they start to turn golden, about 2 minutes, being careful to not burn the peanuts. Reduce the heat to medium. Add the chili bean paste and Sriracha and stir-fry with the peanuts just until fragrant and the oil starts to redden, about 20 seconds.

2. Add the onion and cook until translucent, about 2 minutes. Add the carrot, tofu, ginger, and sugar and stir-fry for another 30 seconds. Add ½ cup of the vegetable broth and cook, stirring constantly, until the liquid has evaporated. Add another ½ cup of the broth and repeat the process. (This allows the peanuts, onions, carrots, and tofu to absorb more flavor.) Finally, add the remaining 4 cups broth and bring to a boil. Reduce the heat to medium-low and simmer for 20 minutes.

3. Meanwhile, bring a medium pot of water to a boil and cook the noodles according to package instructions. Drain and divide into individual bowls.

4. Pour the broth over the noodles. Garnish with the scallions and serve hot.

SPICY MISO RAMEN

SERVES 2 AS A MAIN DISH Of all the ramen broth styles, miso ramen is the youngest form, originating from the northern Japanese island of Hokkaido and gaining popularity only in the 1960s. Now it's found all over Japan and has been exported around the world. It's also a great ramen to make when you don't have hours to simmer a pork bone broth; I use homemade dashi as a soup base, but you can also use chicken stock or vegetable broth.

6 dried shiitake mushrooms

1 large shallot, roughly chopped

3 cloves garlic

1 tablespoon minced or grated fresh ginger

1/2 cup white or yellow miso

1/3 cup Sriracha

3 tablespoons mirin

1 tablespoon sesame oil

2 large eggs

2 tablespoons vegetable oil

1/2 pound ground pork

1/2 teaspoon salt, plus more to taste

4 cups dashi, homemade (page 243) or store-bought, or chicken or vegetable stock

8 ounces fresh ramen, or two 3-ounce packages instant ramen

1 sheet nori, cut into rectangular pieces

2 scallions, thinly sliced

1/2 teaspoon toasted white sesame seeds

1. Soak the shiitake mushrooms in warm water until softened, 15 to 20 minutes. Drain, squeeze out the excess water, discard the stems, and thinly slice the caps.

2. In a food processor or blender, combine the shallot, garlic, ginger, miso, Sriracha, mirin, and sesame oil. Blend until smooth. Set the spicy miso paste aside.

3. Place the eggs in a small saucepan with water to cover by at least 1 inch and bring to a boil. Reduce to a simmer and cook for 8 minutes. Drain and rinse under cold water until cool enough to handle, then peel. Rinse off any bits of shell, slice the eggs in half, and set aside.

4. Heat a wok or large skillet over medium-high heat until a bead of water sizzles and evaporates on contact. Add the vegetable oil and swirl to coat the bottom. Add the pork and stir-fry, breaking it up as much as possible with a spatula, until golden brown and crispy, 5 to 6 minutes. Add the shiitake mushrooms and cook for another 3 minutes to soften. Add the salt. Transfer to a bowl and set aside.

5. In a medium pot, bring the dashi to a simmer. Put the spicy miso paste in a fine-mesh sieve and lower the paste into the stock. Use a spoon to help the miso dissolve into the simmering broth. Discard any solids that remain in the sieve. Adjust the seasoning with salt if needed.

RECIPE CONTINUES

CONTINUED FROM PREVIOUS PAGE

6. Meanwhile, bring a pot of water to a boil and cook the ramen according to package instructions.

7. Divide the ramen into individual bowls and ladle the spicy miso broth on top. Add the pork/mushroom mixture, the hard-boiled eggs, and the nori. Sprinkle with the scallions and sesame seeds and serve.

TIP

For a vegan version of this dish, you can stir-fry crumbled tempeh, chopped seitan, or chopped baked tofu instead of pork.

SRIRACHA TAMARIND PORK

SERVES 4 AS PART OF A MULTICOURSE MEAL This is a twist on one of my favorite dishes, a pork stew from Macau, a former Portuguese colony that was returned to China in 1999. Macanese cuisine is Chinese-Portuguese with influences from around Southeast Asia and other former Portuguese colonies in Africa, Goa, and Brazil. In the making of tamarind pork, the use of olive oil as the cooking fat stems from Europe, while the tamarind paste comes from Southeast Asia, and the shrimp paste is thoroughly Chinese.

What I love about tamarind pork is the very nice balance of tangy, salty, and sweet flavors. Whenever I make it at home, though, I always end up adding Sriracha when serving; it's not traditional, but complements the green chilies in the dish so well! Be sure to have plenty of rice on hand to go with the juicy pork and luscious sauce.

3 tablespoons olive oil or vegetable oil

1 large onion, diced

3 large cloves garlic, minced

1 pound pork shoulder, cut into 1½-inch pieces

3 tablespoons Sriracha

2 tablespoons tamarind paste

1 tablespoon soy sauce

1 teaspoon fish sauce

1 teaspoon shrimp paste

2½ tablespoons light brown sugar

2 cups chicken stock

1 fresh jalapeño or other medium-hot chili, thinly sliced

1. In a large pot, heat 2 tablespoons of the oil over medium heat. Add the onion and garlic and cook until aromatic and slightly softened, about 2 minutes.

2. Add the pork and cook on all sides until the outsides begin to brown.

3. Add the Sriracha, tamarind paste, soy sauce, fish sauce, shrimp paste, and brown sugar and give everything a quick stir. Add the chicken stock and bring to a boil. Reduce the heat to a simmer, cover, and cook for 30 to 40 minutes, until the liquid is reduced by half.

4. Transfer the meat and sauce to a serving bowl. Garnish with the sliced jalapeño and serve.

SRIRACHA FRIED RICE

SERVES 4 AS A SIDE DISH, OR 2 AS A MAIN DISH There are few comfort food dishes as easy to make and economical as fried rice. Like many New Yorkers, I can fall into the trap of regularly grabbing pizza when I'm famished late at night and everything else is closed. Then I learned a few years ago to just make extra rice when I do have the time to cook. Because you can *always* use it for something, whether it's fried rice, congee, or just reheated with other leftovers. Of those three, fried rice might be my favorite. And it also helps you get rid of other leftover meats and vegetables in your fridge. This Sriracha fried rice is vegetarian, but you can easily make it meaty by adding leftover chicken, pork, or beef.

4 cups cooked white or brown rice, refrigerated overnight

2 tablespoons peanut oil or vegetable oil

1 clove garlic, minced

1 teaspoon minced fresh ginger

2 scallions, thinly sliced, white and green parts kept separate

6 fresh shiitake mushrooms, stems removed and caps finely chopped

1/2 cup frozen shelled edamame

3 tablespoons Sriracha

3 tablespoons soy sauce

2 teaspoons sesame oil

1/8 teaspoon freshly ground black or white pepper

1. Break up the cold cooked rice into smaller clumps.

2. Heat a wok or large skillet over medium-high heat until a bead of water sizzles and evaporates on contact. Add the peanut oil and swirl to coat the bottom. Add the garlic, ginger, and scallion whites and cook until just aromatic, about 30 seconds. And the mushrooms and stir-fry for about 1 minute, until softened.

3. Toss in the rice and break up any remaining clumps with a spatula. Add the peas. Continue to stir-fry until the rice starts to turn golden, about 2 minutes. Stir in the Sriracha, soy sauce, sesame oil, and pepper.

4. Transfer the rice to bowls, sprinkle the scallion greens on top, and serve.

SRIRACHA GARLIC BRUSSELS SPROUTS

SERVES 4 AS A SIDE DISH I used to love Brussels sprouts roasted with just a bit of olive oil, salt, and pepper. They were so simple and delicious that I never thought to give them the spicy treatment, until one day when I needed a spicy side dish to go with the Spicy Miso Ramen (page 71) that I was whipping up for dinner. The Brussels sprouts need only 20 to 25 minutes in the oven, and the garlic, chilies, and sauce heat up quickly in the pan before being tossed with the roasted sprouts. The result is perfectly cooked Brussels sprouts with beautifully golden and crispy outsides, accented with smoky, spicy, and garlicky sauce.

They're great as a vegetable side if you're serving a multicourse meal. Or you could do what I sometimes do, which is just sit down and eat an entire bowl for a snack. (You can, too. Nobody's watching.)

2 tablespoons Sriracha

2 tablespoons rice vinegar

1 teaspoon sesame oil

2 teaspoons honey

1 pound Brussels sprouts, trimmed and halved lengthwise

3 tablespoons olive oil

3/4 teaspoon salt

1 tablespoon peanut oil or vegetable oil

8 to 10 dried red chilies, to taste

6 cloves garlic, minced

1. Preheat the oven to 350°F.

2. In a small bowl, combine the Sriracha, rice vinegar, sesame oil, and honey. Stir until the honey is dissolved and set aside.

3. In a large bowl, toss the Brussels sprouts with the olive oil. Spread the sprouts on a large baking sheet and sprinkle the salt on top. Roast until the top and outside leaves are golden and crispy, 20 to 25 minutes.

4. Heat a wok or large skillet over medium-low heat until a bead of water sizzles and evaporates on contact. Add the peanut oil and swirl to coat the bottom. Add the chilies and stir-fry until the chilies have just begun to blacken and the oil is slightly fragrant, about 30 seconds. Add the garlic and cook just until golden but not burnt, another 20 to 30 seconds. Add the Brussels sprouts to the pan and stir for 30 to 60 seconds to coat with the smoky oil and toasted garlic. Quickly transfer the sprouts, chilies, and garlic to a large bowl or plate. Drizzle the Sriracha-vinegar mixture on top and serve.

SRIRACHA SWEET AND SOUR COLESLAW

SERVES 4 TO 6 Sriracha coleslaw is the ideal addition to a summer cookout or other party where spicy wings or barbecue is on the menu. I made this slaw on the mild side as it is intended to be served as a vegetable side, a cooling palate cleanser amongst other spicy dishes, but if you'd like it spicier, by all means double or triple the amount of Sriracha!

To make shredded cabbage without quartering an entire cabbage, carefully pull the cabbage leaves apart; stack 4 to 5 leaves at a time on top of each other and slice into very thin strips with a sharp knife.

3 cups loosely packed shredded savoy cabbage

3 cups loosely packed shredded red cabbage

1 cup grated carrots

3 scallions, chopped

1 cup sliced almonds

1/2 cup mayonnaise

3 tablespoons rice vinegar

2 tablespoons Sriracha

1 1/2 tablespoons honey

1 teaspoon ground cumin

1 teaspoon salt

1/4 teaspoon freshly ground black pepper

1. In a large bowl, combine the savoy cabbage, red cabbage, carrots, scallions, and almonds and toss to mix together.

2. In a small bowl, whisk together the mayonnaise, rice vinegar, Sriracha, honey, cumin, salt, and pepper. Pour the mixture over the coleslaw and toss to coat. Adjust the seasoning with additional Sriracha, salt, and pepper if needed. Serve immediately or chill until serving.

SRIRACHA SEA SALT BROWNIES

MAKES 16 BROWNIES If you've ever tasted mole poblano or a Mexican hot chocolate, you probably already know that the combination of chili and chocolate is pure culinary magic. I first brought these brownies to a family Christmas party years ago and they were a hit with everyone, from my five-year-old niece to ninety-year-old great-aunt. The texture is somewhere between cakey and fudgey. The spice, rather than hitting you immediately, is subtle at first but slowly builds. The brownies will keep for up to 5 days at room temperature or up to 4 months in the freezer, if they don't all get gobbled up first.

1 stick (4 ounces) unsalted butter, cut into 4 or 5 pieces, plus more for greasing the pan

²/₃ cup semisweet chocolate chips

1 cup packed light brown sugar

½ cup granulated sugar

⅓ cup unsweetened cocoa powder

3 large eggs

1 teaspoon vanilla extract

3 tablespoons Sriracha

1 teaspoon flaky sea salt

1¼ cups all-purpose flour

Powdered sugar, for dusting (optional)

1. Preheat the oven to 350°F. Line a 9-inch square baking pan with parchment paper or foil, with enough extra to hang over the edges of the pan. Grease the parchment paper or foil with butter.

2. In a medium saucepan, melt the butter and chocolate chips over low heat, stirring occasionally. Remove from the heat and whisk in the brown sugar, granulated sugar, and cocoa. Stir in the eggs until well incorporated, then stir in the vanilla, Sriracha, and ½ teaspoon of the sea salt. Stir in the flour until evenly blended.

3. Pour the mixture into the prepared pan. Bake for 20 minutes. Remove from the oven and sprinkle the remaining ½ teaspoon sea salt on top. Return to the oven and bake until a toothpick inserted in the middle comes out with just a little bit of batter or moist crumbs, another 10 to 15 minutes. Remove from the oven and let sit for 15 minutes. Carefully use the parchment paper or foil to transfer the brownies to a cooling rack. Cool on the rack for an additional 20 minutes before slicing into 16 brownies. Once the brownies are cooled to room temperature, you may also dust powdered sugar on top.

NAM PRIK PAO

NAM PRIK PAO (THAI CHILI JAM)

MAKES 1½ TO 2 CUPS In Thailand, *nam prik* is the general name for a number of chili-based sauces or pastes used as a condiment or dipping sauce for fish or vegetables. They're made with fresh or dried chilies, and may include lime, garlic, shallots, sugar, and, often, fermented shrimp, fish sauce, or fish paste. One of my favorites, and one of the only in the bunch that is also used as a cooking ingredient, is nam prik pao, also known as Thai chili jam because of the thick texture and slight sweetness and tanginess in an otherwise savory paste.

Nam prik pao devotees have wildly different opinions on what goes into it, how to make it, and the best way to eat it. Most agree, however, on the core ingredients: dried chilies, shallots, garlic, fish sauce, dried shrimp, and a sweetener like palm sugar. Extras are added depending on the region and who's making the nam prik pao. No matter how it's made, it is a staple in any Thai kitchen, and an intoxicating condiment to eat with fried fish, omelets, and boiled vegetables. If you're down for a quick and tasty Thai-style breakfast, try nam prik toast; it's just crisped bread with chili jam slathered on top.

Pao means roasted, and to make nam prik pao, the dried chilies are first roasted to bring out a smoky, funky aroma. In Thailand, roasting is traditionally done over an open fire, but for modern kitchens you can simply caramelize them in a skillet, along with the shallots and garlic. Shrimp paste will add a briny intensity to this powerhouse ingredient, but if you're aiming for a vegetarian version that doesn't skimp on flavor, see Vegan Nam Prik Pao (opposite).

2 tablespoons vegetable oil, plus more for blending if needed

2 cups dried red chilies (60 to 70), preferably Thai spur or Japonés chilies, stemmed

10 cloves garlic, peeled and smashed

3 shallots, roughly chopped

1 tablespoon shrimp paste

¼ cup tamarind paste

3 tablespoons palm sugar or brown sugar

2 teaspoons fish sauce

1. In a large skillet, heat 1 tablespoon oil over medium-low heat. Add the dried red chilies and gently sauté just until aromatic, 1 to 2 minutes. Add the remaining 1 tablespoon oil to the pan. Add the garlic and shallots and gently sauté until softened and very aromatic, 3 to 4 minutes. Add the shrimp paste and cook, stirring, over medium-low heat until aromatic, another 1 minute. Transfer the mixture to a bowl and allow to cool for 5 minutes.

2. Once the chilies, garlic, and shallots have cooled for a bit, transfer them to a food processor. Add the tamarind paste, palm sugar, and fish sauce. Pulse until a thick chunky paste forms, adding 1 to 2 tablespoons vegetable oil if the paste seems too dry to pulse properly.

3. Transfer to a serving dish if using immediately. If saving for later, transfer to a jar and refrigerate. Lasts for up to 1 month.

VEGAN NAM PRIK PAO (THAI CHILI JAM)

MAKES 2 CUPS For this vegan version, I use dried shiitake mushrooms, plus extra roasted shallots and garlic, to imitate the earthiness of dried shrimp and fish sauce. You'll need to soak the mushrooms to rehydrate and soften them and then sauté them in the pan until they're intensely fragrant.

10 dried shiitake mushrooms

3 tablespoons vegetable oil, plus more if needed

2 cups dried red chilies (60 to 70), preferably Thai spur or Japonés chilies, stemmed

12 cloves garlic, peeled and smashed

5 shallots, roughly chopped

1/4 cup tamarind paste

3 tablespoons palm sugar or light brown sugar

1 1/2 teaspoons salt

1. Soak the shiitake mushrooms in warm water until softened, 10 to 15 minutes. Drain, squeeze out the excess water, discard the stems, and finely chop the caps.

2. In a large skillet, heat 2 tablespoons of the oil over medium-low heat. Add the chilies and gently sauté just until aromatic, 1 to 2 minutes. Add the remaining 1 tablespoon oil to the pan. Add the garlic and shallots and gently sauté until golden and very aromatic, 3 to 4 minutes. Add the mushrooms and sauté for another 2 minutes, adding 1 to 2 tablespoons more vegetable oil if the pan seems dry. Transfer the mixture to a bowl and allow to cool for 5 minutes.

3. Once the mixture has cooled a bit, transfer to a food processor. Add the tamarind paste, palm sugar, and salt. Pulse until a smooth paste forms, adding up to 1/4 cup water if the paste seems too dry to pulse properly. Transfer to a serving dish if using immediately. If saving for later, transfer to an airtight jar and refrigerate. Lasts for 2 weeks in the refrigerator.

THAI-STYLE POMELO SALAD WITH SHALLOTS, MINT, AND COCONUT

SERVES 2 TO 4 AS AN APPETIZER The pomelo, a member of the citrus family, is similar to a grapefruit, but much firmer and more fragrant. Despite its super-thick rind and pith, after peeling, the flesh inside resembles a grapefruit. You'll need to remove the membrane of each section and break apart the fruit inside, which will require some patience, but nothing that a little music can't help pass the time with. The dressing, similar to many fruit salad dressings in Thailand, is composed of nam prik pao, chilies, palm sugar, lime juice, fish sauce, coconut, and fresh mint. This beautiful yet simple salad is tangy, savory, sweet, herbal, and spicy all at once and positively addictive. In the US, pomelos are usually in season in the winter, but you can easily use grapefruit as a substitute.

2 pomelos, or 4 grapefruit

1½ tablespoons palm sugar or dark brown sugar

2 fresh bird's eye chilies, finely chopped

1 tablespoon nam prik pao

2 tablespoons fresh lime juice

1 tablespoon fish sauce or soy sauce

½ cup unsweetened coconut flakes

1 tablespoon vegetable oil

1 shallot, thinly sliced

¼ cup fresh mint leaves

½ cup unsalted roasted peanuts, roughly chopped

1. Cut off the ends from the pomelo to give the pomelo a flat surface to stand on. Once the pomelo is stable and you have a steady grip, carefully slice off the peel, pith, and membranes to reveal the pinkish flesh underneath. Use your hands to split open the pomelo into two parts. Peel the pinkish flesh away from the membrane and separate the flesh into bite-size pieces.

2. In a small bowl, whisk the palm sugar and 2 tablespoons water until the sugar is dissolved. Whisk in the chilies, nam prik, lime juice, and fish sauce. Set aside.

3. In a dry skillet, toast the coconut flakes over low heat, being careful not to burn them, until golden, 3 to 4 minutes. Transfer to a bowl and set aside.

4. In the same skillet, heat the vegetable oil over medium-low heat. Add the shallot and fry until golden brown, 2 to 3 minutes. Transfer to a plate lined with paper towels to drain.

5. In a large bowl, toss the pomelo and half the coconut flakes with the nam prik dressing. Toss again with the mint. Top with the fried shallots, peanuts, and the remaining coconut flakes and serve.

SPICY SQUID, CUCUMBER, AND TOMATO SALAD

SERVES 2 TO 4 AS AN APPETIZER Nam prik pao offers an earthy, savory contrast to the light, tangy, and minty flavors in this summery salad. This is also a lightning-fast dish to make; the longest time is spent trimming the squid into bite-size rings and short pieces. One thing to remember is that squid cooks very, very quickly, in just a minute or two, so definitely watch the timer to prevent it from getting rubbery. For variations, try adding sautéed shrimp or baked tofu, and just add a couple minutes to the cooking time

1/2 pound cleaned squid

1 tablespoon fish sauce

1 tablespoon fresh lime juice

2 Persian (mini) cucumbers, or 1 large cucumber, thinly sliced

8 ounces cherry tomatoes, halved

1 small shallot, thinly sliced

1 tablespoon vegetable oil

1 fresh bird's eye or Thai spur chili, minced

2 tablespoons nam prik pao

1/2 cup loosely packed fresh mint leaves

Lime wedges, for serving

1. With a sharp knife or kitchen shears, slice the body of the squid into rings about ½ inch wide. Trim the tentacles into 2- to 3-inch lengths. Pat the squid dry with clean kitchen towels or paper towels.

2. In a large bowl, whisk together the fish sauce and lime juice. Toss the cucumbers, tomatoes, and shallot in the fish sauce mixture and transfer to a serving dish.

RECIPE CONTINUES

3. Heat a wok or large skillet over medium-high heat until a bead of water sizzles and evaporates on contact. Add the oil and swirl to coat the bottom. Add the chili and nam prik pao and stir-fry just until aromatic, 10 to 20 seconds. Add the squid and stir-fry until the edges begin to curl, 1 to 2 minutes. (Squid cook very quickly, so don't leave them in the pan too long or they will develop a rubbery texture.)

4. Remove from the heat and transfer the squid to the cucumbers and tomatoes on the serving dish. Add the mint leaves and give everything a quick toss. Serve with additional lime wedges.

BEAK PERFORMANCE

Chili pepper plants use their natural heat to ward off predators, and mammals find the flavor unbearable. But curiously, chilies have no effect on birds. The birds eat the chilies but don't digest the seeds, which then get dropped (along with natural fertilizer) wherever the birds fly—nature's way of ensuring that chili seeds get spread far and wide. In fact, larger domestic chilies, which don't need help being disseminated, hang down from their plants, hidden under the leaves, but small wild chilies tend to point upward to entice birds to swoop down and consume them.

THAI OMELET (KHAO JIAO)

SERVES 2 It's easy to default to scrambled eggs when cooking up a quick breakfast, but sometimes I like to fry up my eggs Thai-style, creating a golden puffy omelet reminiscent of streetside breakfasts in Bangkok. *Khao jiao*, with a pillowy soft center and light crispy edges, is pretty simple to make, but loaded with flavor from the shallots, fish sauce, lime juice, and nam prik pao at the very end. A bit of rice flour in the batter leads to a crispier omelet without needing too much oil. And don't worry about evenness; a crazy shape with jagged edges is part of the charm.

4 large eggs

2 shallots, finely chopped

2 teaspoons fish sauce

1 teaspoon fresh lime juice

1 tablespoon rice flour or cornstarch

¼ cup peanut oil or vegetable oil

Rice, for serving

2 tablespoons nam prik pao, for serving

1. In a medium bowl, whisk together the eggs, shallots, fish sauce, and lime juice until the mixture is frothy. Add the rice flour slowly and whisk until there are no lumps left. Divide the egg mixture between two bowls.

2. In a large skillet, heat the oil over high heat. Once the oil is hot, add one bowl of the egg mixture in one go and allow it to puff up undisturbed for 30 seconds. Carefully flip the omelet over with tongs or two spatulas and cook for another 20 seconds on the other side. Transfer to a plate and serve with rice and a dish of the nam prik pao. Repeat with the second bowl.

THAI LEMONGRASS AND PRAWN SOUP (TOM YUM GOONG)

SERVES 4 AS AN APPETIZER An iconic Thai soup, *tom yum goong* is my go-to soup when I'm craving hot and sour flavors. Nam prik pao forms the unctuous base for this soup, to which other essential ingredients, including lime, fish sauce, chilies, and kaffir lime leaves, are also added. Contrary to popular belief, most versions of tom yum goong use canned evaporated milk rather than coconut milk. Large shrimp is the classic protein for this soup, but you can also substitute chicken, pork, or tofu.

1 stalk lemongrass, lower part pounded and thinly sliced (see How to Prepare Lemongrass, page 23)

3 thick slices fresh galangal

12 kaffir lime leaves, roughly torn

3 to 4 fresh bird's eye or Thai spur chilies, minced

2 tablespoons nam prik pao

1 pound large shrimp, peeled and deveined

6 ounces straw mushrooms

½ cup canned evaporated milk

1 tablespoon fish sauce

3 tablespoons fresh lime juice (about 2 limes)

Cilantro, for garnish (optional)

1. In a large pot, bring 6 cups water to a boil. Add the lemongrass, galangal, kaffir lime leaves, and chilies and simmer for 5 minutes. Add the nam prik pao and stir until fully dissolved.

2. Add the shrimp and cook, stirring occasionally, for about 1 minute. Add the mushrooms and simmer for another 1 minute. Add the evaporated milk and simmer until the shrimp are pink on the outside and firm inside, another 1 minute. Remove from the heat and stir in the fish sauce and lime juice. Adjust the seasoning with more fish sauce if needed. Transfer to individual bowls for serving and garnish with cilantro if desired.

THAI CHICKEN, COCONUT, AND GALANGAL SOUP (TOM KHA GAI)

SERVES 4 AS AN APPETIZER Along with *tom yum goong*, *tom kha gai* is one of the best known soups in Thai cuisine. It seems like a simple enough chicken soup, but the flavors are so explosive and complex that you'll want to make it over and over again. Many cooks use fresh chilies instead of nam prik pao to spice up this soup, but I find that using the paste instead adds so much depth of flavor, and balances out the lime and coconut so well, that it's now impossible for me to leave it out. When working with coconut milk in a soup, be sure to keep it on a gentle simmer rather than a full boil, and to stir it often (to prevent it from curdling or clumping).

1 stalk lemongrass, lower part pounded and thinly sliced (see How to Prepare Lemongrass, page 23)

8 slices (¼ inch thick) peeled fresh galangal or ginger

1 pound boneless, skinless chicken thighs or breasts, cut into slices ¼ inch thick

Two 13.5-ounce cans full-fat coconut milk

4 ounces oyster mushrooms, straw mushrooms, or button mushrooms

¼ cup bamboo shoots (fresh or canned), thinly sliced

6 kaffir lime leaves

¼ cup nam prik pao

2 tablespoons fish sauce

2 tablespoons fresh lime juice

Cilantro, for garnish (optional)

1. In a large pot, combine the lemongrass, galangal, and 3 cups water and bring to a boil. Add the chicken, reduce to a simmer, and cook until no longer pink, 2 to 3 minutes.

2. Stir in the coconut milk, mushrooms, and bamboo shoots and simmer for 3 minutes, stirring gently and often to prevent the coconut milk from curdling. Reduce the heat to medium-low. Tear the kaffir lime leaves with your hands and add to the pot. Stir in the nam prik pao, fish sauce, and lime juice. Stir and simmer for 1 more minute. Remove from the heat and divide into individual bowls. Garnish with cilantro, if desired, and serve.

SWEET AND SPICY MEATBALLS WITH NAM PRIK PAO

SERVES 4 TO 6 AS AN APPETIZER The streets of Bangkok's Chinatown are a meatball lover's paradise. Vendors sell Chinese-Thai beef or pork meatballs on skewers, in congee, or in noodle soups. For parties at home, single meatball servings make for great appetizers. While nam prik pao is used as a glaze or dip for skewered Thai meatballs, I like to also mix it into the meat so you get all that umami goodness in every bite. For the juiciest meatballs, ask your butcher for a fattier ground pork mix.

1 pound ground pork

3 scallions, finely chopped, plus more for garnish

2 cloves garlic, minced

1 tablespoon minced fresh ginger

¼ cup plus 3 tablespoons nam prik pao

½ teaspoon ground coriander

1 teaspoon salt

¼ teaspoon freshly ground white or black pepper

2 large eggs, beaten

½ cup panko bread crumbs

3 tablespoons vegetable oil

3 tablespoons honey

2 tablespoons rice vinegar

2 tablespoons soy sauce

1 teaspoon toasted white sesame seeds

1. Preheat the oven to 350°F. Line a rimmed baking sheet with parchment paper or foil.

2. In a large bowl, mix together the pork, scallions, garlic, ginger, ¼ cup nam prik pao, the coriander, salt, pepper, eggs, and panko until evenly mixed. With your hands, form the mixture into meatballs the size of golf balls or ping-pong balls (about 1½ inches in diameter).

3. In a large skillet, heat the oil over medium-high heat. Working in batches, brown the meatballs on all sides. Transfer the meatballs to the baking sheet and bake until cooked through, about 15 minutes. Cut one open to check for doneness.

4. Meanwhile, in a small saucepot, combine the remaining 3 tablespoons nam prik pao, honey, rice vinegar, and soy sauce. Simmer over medium heat until the liquid thickens enough to coat the back of a spoon.

5. Once the meatballs are done, transfer to a serving dish. Brush the meatballs with the glaze. If serving as hors d'oeuvres, stick a toothpick in each meatball. Sprinkle the sesame seeds and extra scallions on top and serve.

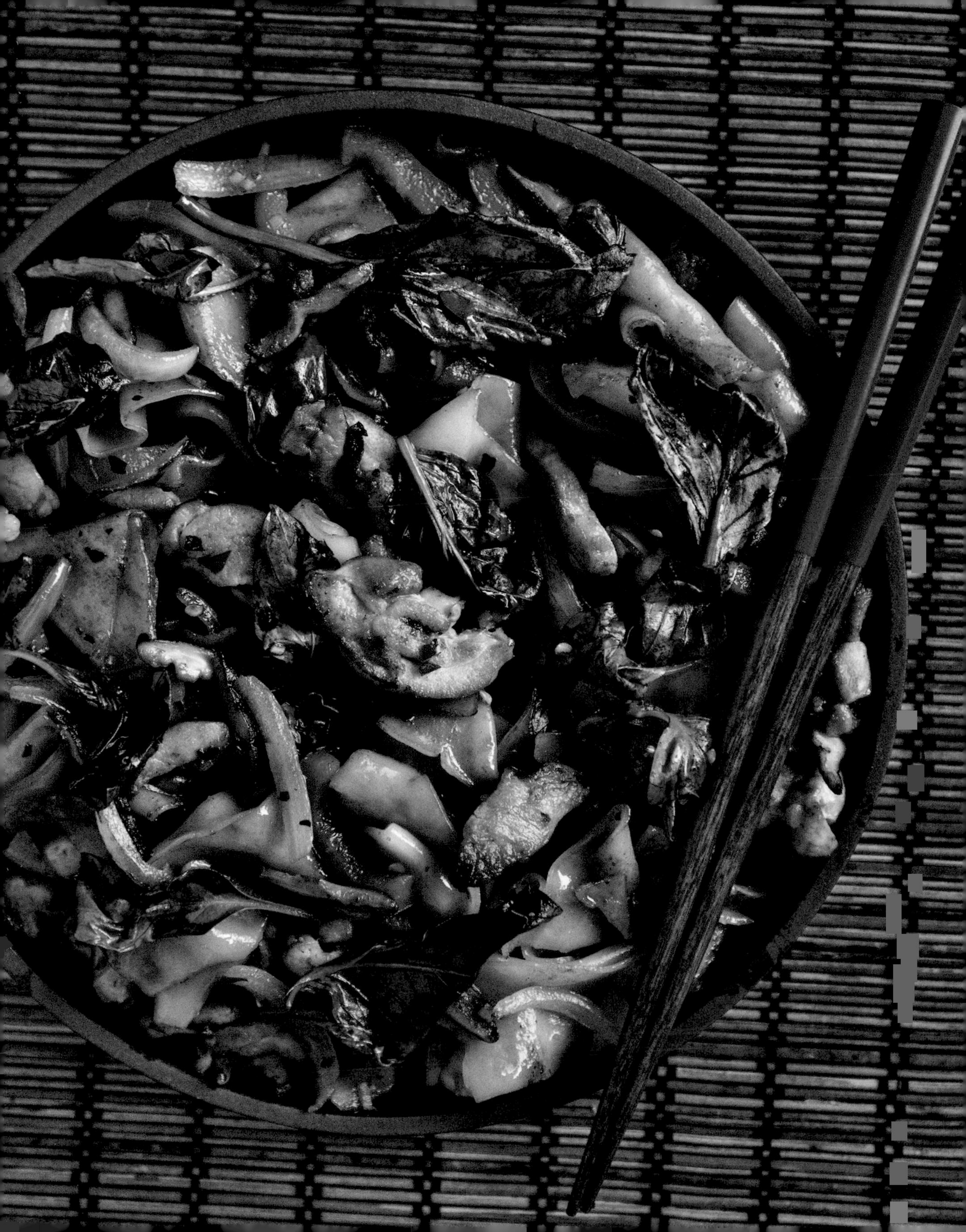

DRUNKEN NOODLES (PAD KEE MAO)

SERVES 4 AS PART OF A MULTICOURSE MEAL, OR 2 OR 3 AS A MAIN DISH If you eat Thai food regularly, you're probably already familiar with drunken noodles, also known as *pad kee mao*. Despite the name, there isn't a drop of alcohol in these noodles; the name instead refers to the idea that this is a dish you crave after a night of drinking. You'll want to look for wide fresh rice noodles, which are available at Chinese and Thai markets and sometimes at stores such as Whole Foods. Normally, the sauce is made with a combination of chilies or Sriracha with oyster sauce, but I like to use nam prik pao, which has roasted spicy, savory, and briny notes that make the noodles even better. You can also replace the chicken with baked tofu for a vegetarian version.

1 pound wide fresh rice noodles

3 tablespoons nam prik pao

1½ tablespoons oyster sauce

1 tablespoon soy sauce

2 teaspoons palm sugar or light brown sugar

3 tablespoons vegetable oil

½ pound boneless, skinless chicken thighs or breasts, cut into bite-size pieces about ¼ inch thick

2 cloves garlic, minced

1 teaspoon minced fresh ginger

2 fresh bird's eye or Thai spur chilies, thinly sliced

1 small onion, thinly sliced

1 red bell pepper, thinly sliced

10 cremini mushrooms, thinly sliced

3 tablespoons vegetable broth or water

2 cups loosely packed fresh Thai basil leaves

Salt

1. In a large bowl, break loose the fresh rice noodles with your hands (this will make them easier to stir-fry later).

2. In a small bowl, whisk together the nam prik pao, oyster sauce, soy sauce, and palm sugar. Set the mixture aside.

3. Heat a wok or large pan over high heat until a bead of water sizzles and evaporates on contact. Add the oil and swirl to coat the bottom. Add the chicken and stir-fry until no longer pink on the outside and cooked through, 3 to 4 minutes. Cut a large piece open to check for doneness. Remove the chicken with a slotted spoon and set aside.

4. In the same wok, stir-fry the garlic, ginger, and chilies until fragrant, about 30 seconds. Add the onion, bell pepper, and mushrooms and stir-fry for 2 minutes. Add the rice noodles and stir-fry until golden around the edges, 3 to 4 minutes. (If the rice noodles start to stick to the bottom of the pan during this time, add a splash of dry sherry or other cooking wine and use a spatula to release the noodles.) Add the broth and simmer for 1 minute, until it is absorbed by the noodles.

5. Return the chicken to the pan. Pour in the nam prik pao sauce, add the Thai basil, and stir so everything gets coated evenly. Adjust the seasoning with salt if needed. Transfer to a large plate and serve.

SPICY LEMONGRASS FRIED RICE

SERVES 4 AS PART OF A MULTICOURSE MEAL, OR 2 OR 3 AS A MAIN DISH The secret to making fried rice is stir-frying with cold leftover rice. Rice that has been chilled overnight is firmer and has less moisture, and develops the signature crispy texture more easily in the wok or pan. Remember to break up your rice into smaller clumps before stir-frying. In a pinch, you can quickly cook a fresh batch of rice, spread a few servings out on a plate, and chill it in the freezer before stir-frying.

4 cups cooked white or brown rice, refrigerated overnight

3 tablespoons nam prik pao

1½ tablespoons fish sauce

2 tablespoons vegetable oil

3 stalks lemongrass, lower part pounded and thinly sliced (see How to Prepare Lemongrass, page 23)

3 fresh bird's eye or Thai spur chilies, thinly sliced

3 scallions, thinly sliced, white and green parts kept separate

8 ounces baked tofu or extra-firm tofu, cut into thin bite-size pieces

2 Kirby or Persian (mini) cucumbers, thinly sliced

1 lime, cut into wedges

Cilantro, for garnish (optional)

1. Break up the cold cooked rice into smaller clumps.

2. In a small bowl, whisk together the nam prik pao and fish sauce and set aside.

3. Heat a wok or large skillet over medium-high heat until a bead of water sizzles and evaporates on contact. Add the oil and swirl to coat the bottom. Add the lemongrass, chilies, and scallion whites and cook just until aromatic, about 30 seconds. Move the aromatics to the side, creating a well in the middle. Toss in the rice and break up any remaining clumps with a spatula. Stir-fry until the rice starts to turn golden, 2 to 3 minutes.

4. Add the tofu and the nam prik pao mixture and stir to mix evenly. Cook for 1 to 2 more minutes, until the tofu is heated through. Transfer to a deep serving dish with the cucumbers and lime wedges on the side. Sprinkle with the scallion greens and cilantro (if using).

THAI BASIL CHICKEN WITH NAM PRIK PAO

SERVES 4 AS PART OF A MULTICOURSE MEAL Nam prik pao is so versatile that you could easily add it to any protein or vegetable and have a flavor-packed stir-fry in just minutes, without needing much else. One of my favorite combinations is chicken with onions and colorful bell peppers, which don't have much flavor on their own, but are a great blank canvas on which the nam prik pao can shine. I like to use bird's eye chilies or Thai spur chilies here, but feel free to use more or less potent peppers. This is an easy recipe that you can adapt with whatever meat and vegetables look freshest at your local market.

2 tablespoons vegetable oil

3 cloves garlic, minced

2 teaspoons grated fresh ginger

2 fresh bird's eye or Thai spur chilies, minced

1 pound boneless, skinless chicken thighs or breasts, cut into 1-inch pieces

1 small yellow onion, thinly sliced

1 red bell pepper, thinly sliced

1 yellow bell pepper, thinly sliced

3 tablespoons nam prik pao

2 tablespoons fish sauce

1 cup loosely packed fresh Thai basil leaves

1. Heat a wok or large skillet over medium-high heat until a bead of water sizzles and evaporates on contact. Add the oil and swirl to coat the bottom. Add the garlic, ginger, and chilies and stir-fry just until aromatic, 10 to 20 seconds. Add the chicken, spread it out evenly, and allow it to sizzle undisturbed for 1 to 2 minutes to get a nice golden sear on the bottom. Once the chicken develops a sear, stir-fry until no longer pink on the outside, another 2 minutes.

2. Add the onion and bell peppers and stir-fry for another minute. Stir in the nam prik, fish sauce, and Thai basil leaves and stir until the chicken is evenly coated with the sauce. Transfer to a plate and serve.

STIR-FRIED CLAMS WITH NAM PRIK PAO

SERVES 4 AS PART OF A MULTICOURSE MEAL These stir-fried clams have become one of my favorite seafood dishes to return to again and again. After cleaning the clams, the dish comes together in under 10 minutes. With so much flavor just from the nam prik pao and juices released from the clams, you'll need few other ingredients for addictive fiery and briny sauce. The Thai basil balances out the earthier flavors with an herbal note and adds a vibrant color to the dish.

2 pounds Manila clams

1½ tablespoons nam prik pao

1 teaspoon fish sauce

2 teaspoons palm sugar or light brown sugar

2 tablespoons vegetable oil

3 cloves garlic, minced

2 fresh bird's eye or Thai spur chilies, thinly sliced

1 cup loosely packed fresh Thai basil leaves

Rice, for serving

1. Discard any clams that have cracks in the shells or do not shut when gently tapped on the counter. Rinse the clams under cold water and scrub the surfaces well with a clean brush or sponge to remove sand. Dry well with a clean kitchen towel.

2. In a small bowl, whisk together the nam prik pao, fish sauce, palm sugar, and ½ cup water until the sugar is dissolved. Set aside.

3. Heat a wok or large skillet over medium-high heat until a bead of water sizzles and evaporates on contact. Add the oil and swirl to coat the bottom. Add the garlic and chilies and stir-fry just until aromatic, 10 to 20 seconds. Add the clams and stir-fry for 30 seconds. Add the nam prik sauce and stir to coat. Cover and steam the clams until they open, 3 to 4 minutes. Uncover and discard any of the clams that did not open. Add the Thai basil, give everything another quick stir, and then transfer to a large serving dish. Serve hot with rice on the side.

COCONUT RED CURRY CHICKEN AND WILD RICE SOUP

SERVES 4 This is one of my favorite soups to throw together on a lazy Sunday. You simmer the chicken thighs in the broth to coax the most flavor from the meat and bones, then shred the meat and cook it with sweet potatoes, zucchini, mushrooms, wild rice, and red curry paste. Also a great slow cooker meal, this soup is intensely aromatic with chilies, lemongrass, and coconut.

2 tablespoons vegetable oil

1 large or 2 medium yellow onions, diced

3 cloves garlic, minced

2 teaspoons minced fresh ginger

8 fresh shiitake or cremini mushrooms, stems removed and caps thinly sliced

3 tablespoons Thai red curry paste

1 pound bone-in, skin-on chicken thighs

1¼ cups wild rice

1 cup full-fat coconut milk

2 tablespoons palm sugar or light brown sugar

1 tablespoon fish sauce

1 medium sweet potato, peeled and diced

2 zucchini, quartered lengthwise and cut crosswise into bite-size pieces

Salt

Cilantro, for garnish (optional)

2 limes, cut into wedges, for serving

1. In a pot or Dutch oven, heat the oil over medium-low heat. Add the onions and sauté until softened and translucent, 2 to 3 minutes. Add the garlic, ginger, and mushrooms and sauté until the mushrooms are softened and just beginning to turn golden, another 2 minutes. Add the red curry paste and cook just until aromatic, about 30 seconds. Add the chicken thighs and 7 cups water and bring to a boil over high heat. Reduce the heat to a simmer and cook for 25 minutes, until the chicken is cooked fully and the liquid has reduced slightly.

2. Transfer the chicken thighs to a plate and allow to cool. Add the wild rice to the pot and stir in the coconut milk, palm sugar, and fish sauce. Simmer for 15 minutes. Add the sweet potato and simmer until the wild rice and sweet potato are cooked through, another 20 minutes.

3. Meanwhile, shred the chicken thighs with your hands and discard the bones (you may discard the skin if you'd like but I like to keep it for flavor).

4. Add the zucchini to the pot and simmer, stirring occasionally, until the zucchini is cooked through, another 5 minutes. Return the chicken to the pot for another 1 minute to heat through. Adjust the seasoning with salt if needed. Divide into individual bowls, garnish with cilantro (if using), and serve with lime wedges on the side.

THAI RED CURRY BUTTERNUT SQUASH SOUP

SERVES 4 AS AN APPETIZER On Sunday nights in the fall, I often make a large batch of butternut squash soup ready to heat up for the coming week. It's great for those chilly days when you just need something warming, or when you're feeling slightly under the weather. And this isn't your run-of-the-mill butternut squash soup either. The red curry paste adds a kick as well as a deep earthiness, and the coconut milk makes the soup extra fragrant. Feel free to add any vegetables or protein to turn this soup into a main dish.

2 tablespoons coconut oil or vegetable oil

1 small yellow onion, diced

2 tablespoons Thai red curry paste

2 pounds butternut squash, peeled, seeded, and cut into 2-inch pieces

2 cups vegetable broth

One 13.5-ounce can full-fat coconut milk

1 teaspoon ground coriander

1 teaspoon crushed red chili flakes

Salt

Lime wedges, for serving

Handful of mint or cilantro, for garnish

1. In a large pot, heat the coconut oil over low heat. Add the onion and cook over low heat until soft and translucent, 5 to 6 minutes. Add the red curry paste and sauté until fragrant, 1 to 2 minutes. Add the butternut squash and vegetable broth. Bring the broth to a boil, then reduce the heat and simmer until the butternut squash is very soft, 20 to 25 minutes.

2. Allow the broth to cool for 5 to 10 minutes. Working in batches, blend the soup in a blender until smooth. Transfer the soup to a clean pot and bring to a simmer. Stir in the coconut milk, coriander, and chili flakes and simmer for 3 to 4 minutes to blend the flavors. Season with salt to taste. Transfer to individual bowls and serve with lime wedges and garnish with mint or cilantro.

THAI ZUCCHINI, YELLOW SQUASH, AND EGGPLANT CURRY

SERVES 4 TO 6 AS PART OF A MULTICOURSE MEAL This vegetarian curry is perfect for summer and early fall when zucchini, yellow squash, and eggplant are in season. It's so quick and easy to throw together that it can become a weeknight standby. The vegetables take only about 8 minutes to cook, and act as a sponge for the tasty sauce of red curry and coconut milk. You can also make the dish fully vegetarian by substituting soy sauce for the fish sauce, but I love the earthiness that the fish sauce adds. The Thai basil goes in toward the end, and adds a refreshing herbal note.

3 tablespoons vegetable oil

1 medium onion, diced

1 bell pepper, diced

2 cloves garlic, minced

1 teaspoon minced or grated fresh ginger

1/4 cup Thai red curry paste

Two 13.5-ounce cans full-fat coconut milk

1 1/2 tablespoons fish sauce or soy sauce

1 tablespoon palm sugar or light brown sugar

1 pound zucchini, cut into half-moons about 1/2 inch thick

1 pound yellow squash, cut into half-moons about 1/2 inch thick

1 pound Asian eggplant, cut into half-moons about 1/2 inch thick

1 cup loosely packed fresh Thai basil leaves

Salt

1. In a large deep sauté pan or a Dutch oven, heat the oil over medium-high heat. Add the onion and bell pepper and sauté until softened all around, 2 to 3 minutes. Add the garlic, ginger, and curry paste and cook until aromatic, another minute.

2. Pour in the coconut milk and bring the liquid to a simmer. Stir in the fish sauce and palm sugar. Add the yellow squash, zucchini, and eggplant and simmer uncovered until the vegetables are very tender, 8 to 10 minutes.

3. Stir in the Thai basil leaves and cook for another minute. Adjust the seasoning with salt if needed. Transfer to a deep serving dish and serve.

CHIANG MAI PORK BELLY CURRY

SERVES 4 AS PART OF A MULTICOURSE MEAL This specialty from Northern Thailand is sometimes called Burmese Curry, adopted from the country that occupied the region for hundreds of years. Unlike most Thai curries, this version uses no coconut milk, but is instead intensely fragrant with red curry paste, cumin, cinnamon, fish sauce, and tamarind paste. The explosive flavors balancing hot, sour, salty, and sweet make this an easy crowd-pleaser. Pork belly is the go-to protein to use for this curry, but you can also substitute pork shoulder if you'd prefer a leaner cut. This dish is easy to make in large volumes and you can easily double or triple the amounts. Rice and a side salad would go excellent with the curry.

¼ cup Thai red curry paste

1 tablespoon ground cumin

1 teaspoon ground cinnamon

1 teaspoon ground coriander

1 teaspoon paprika

2 tablespoons fish sauce

2 tablespoons tamarind paste

2 tablespoons palm sugar or 1 tablespoon brown sugar

2 tablespoons vegetable oil

2 pounds pork belly, cut into bite-size cubes

2 large shallots, thinly sliced

5 cloves garlic, minced

½ tablespoon minced or grated fresh ginger

2 stalks lemongrass, lower part pounded and thinly sliced (see How to Prepare Lemongrass, page 23)

Salt

1. In a small bowl, stir together the Thai red curry paste, cumin, cinnamon, coriander, and paprika. In another small bowl, combine the fish sauce, tamarind paste, and palm sugar (you do not need to stir). Set both bowls aside.

2. Heat a wok, heavy-bottomed pot, or large skillet over medium heat until a bead of water added to the skillet sizzles. Add the vegetable oil and swirl to coat the bottom. Add the pork belly and sear until golden brown on the outside, 2 to 3 minutes. Add the shallots, garlic, ginger, and lemongrass and cook until aromatic and the shallots have softened, 1 to 2 minutes. Add the Thai curry paste mixture and stir-fry for 1 minute. Add 3 cups water, stir in the fish sauce mixture, and bring to a simmer. Simmer the pork until it is meltingly tender and the sauce is thick enough to coat the back of a spoon, 50 to 60 minutes. Adjust the seasoning with salt if needed. Transfer to a serving dish and serve with rice and salad.

CUMIN-CRUSTED RED CURRY RACK OF LAMB

SERVES 4 AS PART OF A MULTICOURSE MEAL Whether it's served at a small intimate dinner or a large party, this red curry rack of lamb is a showstopper. It's inspired by a cumin-crusted rack of lamb at one of my favorite Chinese restaurants in Queens, New York, and I wanted to try a red curry paste rub because the deep, earthy flavors in the paste pairs so well with whole cumin and lamb. It's also much less complex to make than it seems. Simply season the lamb, pat the red curry and bread crumb mixture on top, and roast for about half an hour. While it cooks in the oven, you have plenty of time and counter space to prepare your sides and dessert.

3 tablespoons cumin seeds

1/3 cup panko or regular bread crumbs

1/4 cup Thai red curry paste

1 tablespoon vegetable oil

One 8-rib rack of lamb (1 1/2 to 2 pounds), Frenched

Salt and freshly ground black pepper

1. Preheat the oven to 400°F.

2. In a small skillet, toast the cumin seeds until aromatic, 30 to 60 seconds. In a small bowl, combine the toasted cumin seeds, panko, curry paste, and oil. Season the rack of lamb all over with salt and pepper. Pat the crumb mixture evenly over the fat side and arrange the rack of lamb crumb side up in a roasting pan.

3. Roast the lamb until a meat thermometer stuck in the thickest part of the meat registers 135° for medium-rare or 145°F for medium, 25 to 30 minutes. (If the bread crumbs start to brown too much, loosely cover the rack of lamb with foil.) Carefully transfer to a cutting board, cover the top with foil, and let it rest for 10 minutes (the internal temperature will rise slightly as it rests). Cut the lamb into pieces by slicing between the bones and serve.

THAI RED CURRY CHICKEN AND GREEN BEAN STIR-FRY (GAI PAD PRIK GAENG)

SERVES 4 AS PART OF A MULTICOURSE MEAL One of my favorite Thai street foods, *gai pad prik gaeng*, is an easy dish to re-create at home if you have Thai red curry paste on hand. The chicken and green beans stir-fry in just minutes. And because the curry paste is already aromatic with chilies, lemongrass, and galangal, you don't need a lot of other flavorings. The green beans are meant to be crisp-tender and need only 2 minutes of cooking time.

2 tablespoons high-heat cooking oil, such as peanut oil or vegetable oil

3 tablespoons Thai red curry paste

1 pound boneless, skinless chicken thighs, cut into 1-inch pieces

1/2 pound green beans, trimmed and cut into 1 1/2-inch lengths

1 teaspoon fish sauce

1 teaspoon sugar

5 kaffir lime leaves

1. In a large wok or skillet, heat the oil over medium heat. Add the curry paste and stir-fry until fragrant, about 30 seconds. Add the chicken and spread on the pan in a single layer; leave it alone for 1 to 2 minutes to get a nice sear. When the bottom starts to turn golden, continue stirring for 2 to 3 minutes, until the chicken is no longer pink on the outside.

2. Add the green beans and cook for 1 minute. Stir in the fish sauce and sugar. Tear the kaffir lime leaves into large pieces and add them to the mixture. Stir until the chicken is cooked through, another 1 minute. Transfer to a large plate or bowl and serve.

THAI RED CURRY MUSSELS

SERVES 4 AS PART OF A MULTICOURSE MEAL When I make mussels at home, they're usually steamed with a minimal number of other ingredients, such as wine and garlic. But sometimes I like to spice things up a bit (pun fully intended) by cooking it Thai-style with red curry paste. The coconut milk and lime make this the quintessential summer dish. A bit of lime juice, coconut milk, fish sauce, and palm sugar create a lip-smacking sweet and sour curry.

You'll need to clean the mussels in several changes of water (a clean brush comes in handy for scrubbing the shells) and also pull the beards from the shells. But the cooking itself takes all of 5 or 6 minutes. There will be plenty of delicious curry left, so be sure to have white rice to pour the broth over or crusty French bread for dipping.

2 pounds mussels

1 tablespoon peanut oil or vegetable oil

2 cloves garlic, minced

1 tablespoon minced fresh ginger

3 tablespoons Thai red curry paste

One 13.5-ounce can coconut milk

2 tablespoons fish sauce

2 tablespoons palm sugar or light brown sugar

Salt and freshly ground black pepper (optional)

3 limes, cut into wedges, for serving

1. Rinse and scrub the mussels under cold water, changing the water several times, to remove any grit. Debeard the mussels by pulling the stringy bits out from between the two shells near the hinge as best you can. Discard any mussels with cracked shells or any with open shells that don't close when you gently tap them against the counter.

2. Heat a deep sauté pan, wok, or medium pot over medium-high heat until a bead of water sizzles and evaporates on contact. Add the oil and swirl to coat the bottom. Add the garlic and ginger and cook briefly until aromatic, 20 to 30 seconds. Add the curry paste and cook for another 30 to 40 seconds.

3. Add the coconut milk, fish sauce, and palm sugar and bring the liquid to a boil. Add the mussels, cover, and steam, shaking the pan occasionally, until the mussels open, 4 to 5 minutes. Uncover and discard any mussels that have not opened.

4. Season with salt and pepper if desired, then transfer the mussels to a serving dish. Spoon the curry over the mussels and add lime wedges to the dish (for squeezing at the table).

CAULIFLOWER STEAKS WITH RED CURRY PEANUT SAUCE

SERVES 4 AS PART OF A MULTICOURSE MEAL If you've never had cauliflower "steaks" before, this vegetarian side is exactly as it sounds—cauliflower sliced into flat steaks that you can grill, roast, or pan-fry. I prefer roasting because it cooks the cauliflower most evenly, and you end up with slightly crisp and golden brown edges while the middle stays tender. The Thai red curry peanut sauce makes a lovely spicy and creamy sauce to drizzle over the steaks.

1 head cauliflower

3 tablespoons olive oil

1/2 teaspoon salt

1 1/2 cups full-fat coconut milk, soy milk, or almond milk

2 tablespoons Thai red curry paste

3 tablespoons peanut butter

1 teaspoon sugar

1/4 cup unsalted dry-roasted peanuts, chopped

1/4 cup roughly chopped cilantro (optional)

1. Preheat the oven to 350°F. Line a baking sheet with parchment paper or foil.

2. Carefully trim the outer leaves off the cauliflower while leaving the stem intact. Place the cauliflower on the cutting board, stem side down. With a chef's knife, slice the cauliflower vertically into 4 slabs about 1 inch thick all the way through the stem. Reserve about 2 cups of loose florets for the sauce; any remaining loose florets can be saved for another use.

3. Rub the cauliflower steaks with the oil and lay them on the baking sheet in a single layer. Sprinkle the salt over the top. Roast until golden brown and slightly crispy around the edges, 35 to 40 minutes.

4. In a food processor, pulse together the reserved 2 cups cauliflower florets until it resembles the texture of couscous. Add the coconut milk, red curry paste, peanut butter, and sugar and blend until a smooth paste forms.

5. Heat a small saucepan over medium heat. Add the curry paste mixture. Simmer until the sauce is thick enough to coat the back of a spoon, 2 to 3 minutes.

6. Transfer the cauliflower steaks to a large serving dish or divide among four plates. Drizzle the red curry peanut sauce over the steaks, and garnish with the peanuts and cilantro (if using). Serve with rice on the side.

SWEET CHILI SAUCE

SWEET CHILI SAUCE

MAKES ABOUT 1½ CUPS Known as *nam chim kai* in Thai, sweet chili sauce is remarkably easy to DIY at home. While glass-bottled versions from Thailand are widely available in Southeast Asian and Chinese markets in the US, I like being able to control the amount of sweetness and heat in a sauce I use almost every day. Plus, you can find all the ingredients at your local market, and there are no additives or preservatives.

You can use it in dips for appetizers like summer rolls and fried tofu, glazes for chicken or fish, and even salad dressings and desserts. I love using it plain as a dip for raw vegetables or dumplings, a fiery alternative to hummus and soy sauce, respectively. The sweetness is easy to control by varying the amount of sugar, and the heat by choosing the type of chilies you use. Red jalapeños or Fresnos are my favorite because they give a medium heat closest to store-bought versions of sweet chili sauce. If you use spicier chilies like serranos or Thai spurs, you will need to double or triple the number of chilies to produce the same volume and color (and take out the seeds unless you prefer a flaming hot sauce!). You can also experiment with other fresh chilies that you come across. If you'd like to kick up the umami flavor, add a couple drops of fish sauce to your batch. Feel free to double, triple, or even quadruple the recipe.

5 fresh red jalapeño or Fresno chilies, roughly chopped

1 clove garlic, peeled

½ cup rice vinegar

½ cup sugar

½ teaspoon salt

1 tablespoon cornstarch

1. In a food processor, combine the chilies, garlic, rice vinegar, sugar, salt, and ½ cup water and blend until pureed.

2. Transfer the mixture to a medium skillet and bring to a boil. Reduce to a simmer and cook for 3 to 5 minutes, until the liquid is slightly reduced. Whisk the cornstarch with 2 tablespoons water until the cornstarch is completely dissolved, then stir it into the chili pepper mixture. Cook, stirring, until the mixture has thickened, another 30 to 60 seconds. Transfer to a bowl to cool and use immediately or store in an airtight container in the fridge. The refrigerated sweet chili sauce will keep for up to 1 month.

CRISPY TOFU WITH SWEET CHILI PEANUT SAUCE

SERVES 4 AS AN APPETIZER This popular street food in Thailand makes a great afternoon snack or vegetarian appetizer to serve at parties. Use firm or extra-firm tofu for the best results; the triangles should be crunchy on the outside but pillowy on the inside once they fry up. I like to thin out the sweet chili sauce to incorporate it with the soy sauce, but the sauce will thicken again once it cools.

1 block firm or extra-firm tofu, drained and rinsed

2 teaspoons salt

2 tablespoons sweet chili sauce

½ tablespoon soy sauce or fish sauce

3 tablespoons chopped unsalted dry-roasted peanuts

Vegetable oil, for deep-frying

1 scallion, chopped

1. Cut the tofu vertically into 1-inch-thick slabs and dry very well on all sides with clean kitchen towels. (This will prevent the oil from sputtering when the tofu goes into hot oil.) Slice each slab into triangles. Sprinkle the salt over the tofu.

2. In a small saucepan, stir together the sweet chili sauce, soy sauce, and 2 tablespoons water over low heat until the sweet chili sauce is evenly thinned out, 1 to 2 minutes. Remove from the heat and stir in the peanuts. Transfer to a bowl to cool.

3. Pour about 2 inches vegetable oil into a wok or heavy-bottomed pot and heat until the temperature reads 350°F on a deep-fry thermometer. Working in batches, fry the tofu until golden brown, 3 to 4 minutes. Use tongs to separate the tofu if it starts to stick together. Transfer to a plate lined with paper towels to drain and continue with the rest of the batches.

4. Once all the tofu is fried, transfer to a serving dish. Sprinkle the chopped scallion over the cooled dipping sauce and serve.

TATSOI AND ROMAINE SALAD WITH BLOOD ORANGE AND SWEET CHILI DRESSING

SERVES 4 AS AN APPETIZER OR SIDE DISH Tatsoi is a versatile leafy green that can be eaten in salads, stir-fries, or soups. In late fall or early winter, when tatsoi is in season in the Northeast, I like to make a salad with blood oranges and carrots from the farmers' market, a colorful dish to brighten up the shortening days. The sweet chili sauce and blood orange juice in the dressing provide a zingy flavor that pairs well with the mild mustardy flavor of the tatsoi.

4 blood oranges

1 tablespoon sweet chili sauce

2 teaspoons honey or agave nectar

1 teaspoon grated fresh ginger

3 tablespoons extra-virgin olive oil

1 small bunch tatsoi, thick stems removed (about 4 cups loosely packed leaves)

4 cups loosely packed baby romaine leaves

1 shallot, thinly sliced

1/4 cup grated carrots (1 to 2 carrots)

2 teaspoons toasted sesame seeds

1. Supreme the oranges: Slice the tops and bottoms from 3 of the oranges. One at a time, stand an orange on a flat surface and slice away the rind and pith from top to bottom, following the curve of the fruit. Hold the oranges over a large bowl, pull the segments away from the membranes, and allow the segments to drop into the bowl.

2. Squeeze the remaining blood orange to get about 1/4 cup juice. Whisk the juice with the sweet chili sauce, honey, ginger, and olive oil.

3. In a large bowl, toss together the tatsoi, baby romaine, orange segments, shallot slices, and grated carrot. Toss with the dressing. Transfer to a serving dish and garnish with sesame seeds.

SPICY MANGO AND TOFU SUMMER ROLLS

SERVES 4 TO 6 AS AN APPETIZER Vietnamese summer rolls may seem intimidating to make, but they're actually quite easy. For these mango summer rolls, you'll need mangoes, tofu, mint, and fresh vegetables that can be cut into strips such as carrots and cucumbers. You'll also need rice paper wrappers and some rice vermicelli noodles, both available in any large Asian market. The rice vermicelli noodles get soaked in hot water to soften, then are laid on top of the soaked rice wrapper along with the fresh ingredients. Summer rolls are best eaten fresh right after they're rolled, but they can be kept at room temperature or refrigerated for up to 2 hours. Sweet chili sauce adds a mellow bite to the peanut dipping sauce.

4 ounces dried rice vermicelli noodles

2 tablespoons peanut butter

2 tablespoons sweet chili sauce

1 tablespoon soy sauce

2 teaspoons honey

2 teaspoons rice vinegar

1 package round rice paper wrappers

8 ounces baked tofu, cut into thin strips

1 large carrot, julienned

1 large cucumber, julienned

1 large mango, peeled and cut into strips

24 mint leaves

1. Bring a small pot of water to a boil. Place the rice vermicelli noodles in a large heatproof bowl and pour the just-boiled water over the noodles. Allow the noodles to soak for about 3 minutes. Drain, rinse under cold water, and drain again. (Alternatively, soak the noodles in warm water for 20 to 25 minutes.)

2. In a small bowl, whisk together the peanut butter and 2 tablespoons water until the peanut butter thins out. Whisk in the sweet chili sauce, soy sauce, honey, and rice vinegar. Set the peanut dip aside.

3. Fill a large bowl with room-temperature water.

4. Dip a rice paper wrapper in the water for 30 to 40 seconds, making sure all sides are wet and the wrapper is very softened. Lay the wrapper flat on a cutting board or other clean surface. Lay a small bunch of vermicelli noodles in the bottom one-third of the wrapper. Lay strips of tofu, carrot, cucumber, and mango horizontally over the noodles. Top with 2 mint leaves.

5. Fold the bottom of the rice paper over the filling and begin rolling tightly. Fold the left and right sides of the wrapper over the filling. Finish rolling tightly. Lay the finished summer roll seam side down on a plate and cover with a slightly damp towel. Repeat with the remaining wrappers and filling.

6. Serve the mango summer rolls with the peanut dip on the side.

SWEET CHILI BAKED STUFFED MUSHROOMS

SERVES 4 AS AN APPETIZER OR SIDE DISH When I was growing up, Chinese-style baked stuffed mushrooms were a fixture at the Chinese buffets my family frequented in suburban Massachusetts. Usually filled with a sesame-accented pork filling that became caramelized in the oven, these bite-size morsels were hard to resist. In this spicy version, you can use either the more traditional ground pork or panko crumbs for a vegetarian take. Done in just 20 minutes, the mushrooms make tasty hors d'oeuvres for parties or a great side dish at dinner. You can also mix the filling and stuff the mushrooms ahead of time, then just pop them in the oven before serving.

FILLING

½ pound ground pork (use 1¼ cups panko bread crumbs for vegetarian)

2 teaspoons minced fresh ginger

2 scallions, finely chopped

¼ cup sweet chili sauce

2 tablespoons soy sauce

2 tablespoons sesame oil

MUSHROOMS

12 ounces cremini or white button mushrooms

3 tablespoons olive oil

2 teaspoons white sesame seeds

1. Preheat the oven to 350°F. Line a baking sheet with parchment paper or foil.

2. Make the filling: In a small bowl, combine the pork (or panko), ginger, scallions, sweet chili sauce, soy sauce, and sesame oil. Mix thoroughly; the filling should resemble a thick paste. Set aside.

3. Prepare the mushrooms: Remove and discard the stems from the mushrooms and wipe the caps with a slightly damp towel. Fill the mushroom caps with about 1 tablespoon of filling. Pack tightly so the top of the filling is rounded like a miniature dome. Place the stuffed mushrooms on the prepared baking sheet, stuffing side up. With a pastry brush, brush the top of the filling and the sides of the mushrooms with the olive oil. Sprinkle the sesame seeds on top.

4. Bake until the pork is cooked through, about 20 minutes (for the vegetarian version, bake until the mushrooms are golden, 15 to 20 minutes). Remove from the oven and allow the mushrooms to cool for a few minutes before serving. Serve warm or at room temperature.

SWEET CHILI LIME CHICKEN

SERVES 4 AS PART OF A MULTICOURSE MEAL This is an entree that disappears quickly whenever I serve it at potluck dinner parties. It's difficult to say which part is more addictive—the crunchy and airy texture, or the flavors of sweet chili sauce mixed with freshly squeezed lime juice. The shallow-frying method in the recipe will produce the same crisp texture as deep-frying without using a lot of oil, and you have the option of getting the chicken extra crunchy by double-frying for 30 extra seconds.

2 tablespoons soy sauce

2 egg whites

1 pound boneless, skinless chicken thighs or breasts, cut into 1-inch cubes

6 tablespoons sweet chili sauce

2 tablespoons Chinese rice wine or dry sherry

1 tablespoon fresh lime juice

1 teaspoon sesame oil

1/2 teaspoon crushed red chili flakes

1 1/2 cups cornstarch

1/2 teaspoon salt

1/4 teaspoon freshly ground black pepper

3 cups plus 1 tablespoon peanut oil or vegetable oil

8 dried red chilies (Japonés, serrano, Tien Tsin, or cayenne)

3 cloves garlic, minced

1 teaspoon minced fresh ginger

1 teaspoon white sesame seeds, for garnish

Scallions, green parts thinly sliced, for garnish

1. In a large bowl, combine the soy sauce and egg whites. Add the chicken, toss to coat with the mixture, and let sit for 10 minutes.

2. In a small bowl, combine the sweet chili sauce, rice wine, lime juice, sesame oil, and chili flakes. Set the sauce aside.

3. In a large bowl or deep plate, toss the cornstarch with the salt and black pepper. Add the chicken and toss to coat in the cornstarch, shaking off any excess before frying.

4. Pour the 3 cups of oil into a wok and heat until the temperature reads 350°F on a deep-fry thermometer. Working in two or three batches, fry the chicken cubes until golden brown on the outside and cooked through, 4 to 5 minutes, flipping with tongs about halfway through to ensure even cooking. Transfer the chicken to a plate lined with paper towels to drain. Optional: To get the chicken extra crispy, work in batches again and return the chicken to the oil for 30 more seconds before draining again on paper towels.

RECIPE CONTINUES

SWEET CHILI QUINOA SALAD WITH BLACK BEANS AND CHERRY TOMATOES

SERVES 4 This is one of my favorite lunches to pack for a road trip, especially in the summer when tomato season is at its peak. There's an interesting textural mix of slightly crunchy quinoa, soft black beans, and juicy cherry tomatoes, punctuated by the alluring scent of lightly cooked chilies, shallots, and cumin. It's gently spiced but flavorful, light but filling, exactly what I need when venturing off for a hike or day at the beach.

1½ cups quinoa, rinsed

2 tablespoons olive oil

3 shallots, thinly sliced

Two 15- or 16-ounce cans black beans, rinsed and drained

¼ cup sweet chili sauce

2 teaspoons ground cumin

2 teaspoons salt, plus more to taste

1 pound cherry tomatoes, halved

¼ teaspoon freshly ground black pepper

A small handful of chopped mint (optional)

1. In a pot, combine the quinoa and 2½ cups water. Bring to a boil, then reduce to a simmer and cook, covered, until the water is absorbed and the quinoa is fluffy, about 15 minutes.

2. In a skillet, heat 1 tablespoon of the olive oil over low heat. Add the shallots and sauté until aromatic and softened, 1 to 2 minutes. Add the drained black beans, sweet chili sauce, cumin, and 2 teaspoons salt, stir, and cook for 1 minute more.

3. Transfer the quinoa to a large bowl. Add the black bean/shallot mixture, cherry tomatoes, remaining 1 tablespoon olive oil, black pepper, and salt to taste. Mix well. Taste and adjust the seasoning with salt and pepper if you'd like. Garnish with mint (optional). The quinoa can be served warm or at room temperature.

SWEET CHILI BOK CHOY

SERVES 4 AS A SIDE DISH One of the most important things to know about stir-frying bok choy and other leafy greens is that they should only cook for 2 to 3 minutes in the wok or pan. A super-short cooking time allows the leaves to stay crisp-tender with a distinctive crunch. For this stir-fry, the leaves of the baby bok choy are small enough to be left whole; just trim off 1/4 inch or so of hard stem on the bottom. The sweet chili sauce gives the bok choy a light spiciness, and the sesame oil drizzled at the end adds a nice toasted aroma.

1 1/2 pounds baby bok choy

3 tablespoons sweet chili sauce

1 teaspoon soy sauce

1 tablespoon Chinese rice wine or dry sherry

1/2 teaspoon sugar

2 tablespoons vegetable oil

1 clove garlic, minced

One 1-inch piece fresh ginger, peeled and minced

2 teaspoons sesame oil

1. Trim the rough bottoms from the baby bok choy and separate the leaves. Rinse and pat the leaves very dry (even a little bit of water will cause the oil to spit in the pan).

2. In a small bowl, combine the sweet chili sauce, soy sauce, rice wine, and sugar. Set the sauce aside.

3. Heat a wok over high heat until a bead of water sizzles and evaporates on contact. Add the vegetable oil and swirl to coat the bottom. Add the garlic and ginger and stir-fry until aromatic, 10 to 20 seconds. Add the bok choy and stir-fry until the stems are slightly tender but still a little crisp, about 2 minutes. Add the sauce mixture and cook for another 30 seconds. Remove from the heat, drizzle with the sesame oil, then immediately transfer to a serving plate.

COCONUT GRANITA
WITH ROASTED SWEET CHILI CASHEWS

SERVES 4 Looking for a refreshing dessert with a kick? Try this coconut granita, with spicy candied cashews paired with creamy coconut ice. Granita is an Italian frozen dessert like a shaved ice or slushy, but you can make it even without any fancy equipment. Easy to make and even easier to savor, it's bound to be a staple in your freezer all summer long.

CASHEWS

2 tablespoons sweet chili sauce

2 tablespoons sugar

$1/8$ teaspoon salt

$1/2$ cup raw cashews

GRANITA

$1/2$ cup sugar

One 13.5-ounce can full-fat coconut milk

1. Preheat the oven to 350°F. Line a baking sheet with parchment paper or foil.

2. Prepare the cashews: In a medium bowl, whisk together the sweet chili sauce, sugar, and salt. Toss the cashews with the mixture until well coated. Spread the cashew mixture on the baking sheet in a single layer. Bake, stirring occasionally, until golden, 12 to 15 minutes. Transfer the cashews to a plate lined with foil or parchment. Cool for 10 minutes, then separate and break apart any nut clusters.

3. Make the granita: In a small saucepan, heat $1/2$ cup water over medium heat. Add the sugar and stir until melted to form a simple syrup. Remove from the heat and cool for 10 to 15 minutes.

4. In a large shallow glass baking dish (or other large shallow dish with sides at least 2 inches high), combine the simple syrup and coconut milk, whisking to smooth out any lumps. Place in the freezer and chill for 3 to 4 hours, breaking up or scraping the surface with a spoon every 30 minutes until you have a snowy, flaky consistency. Carefully stir in the sweet chili cashews.

5. Divide the granita and cashews among four bowls or shallow glasses and serve cold.

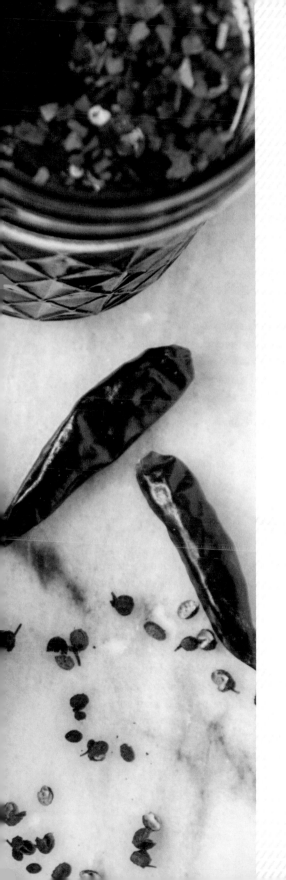

SICHUAN CHILI OIL

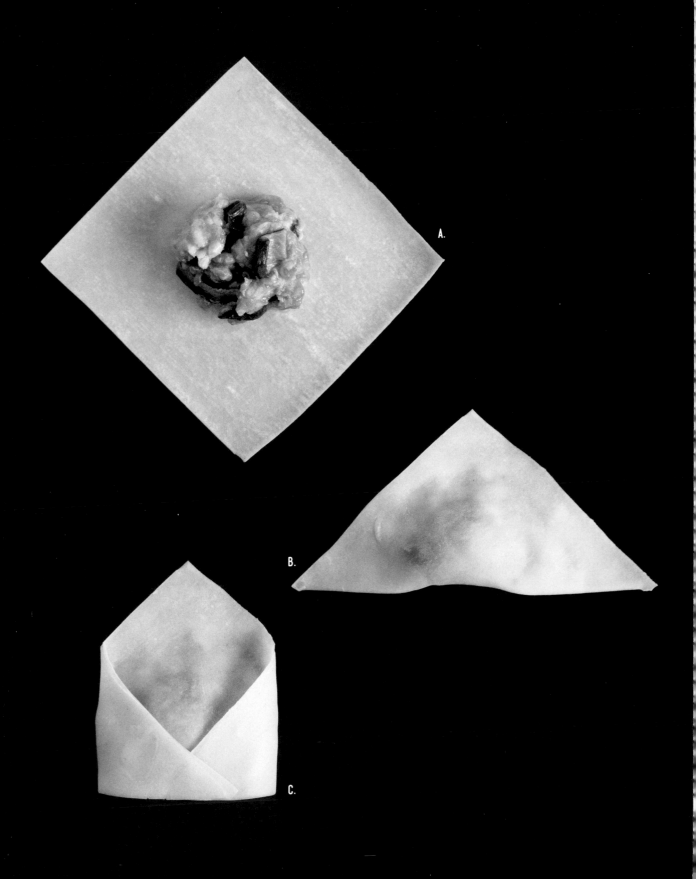

A.

B.

C.

SICHUAN WONTONS

SERVES 4 TO 6 If you've never had Sichuan wontons before, and you're a big fan of spicy food, this is one dish that will surely become a part of your regular rotation. The Mandarin name for Sichuan wontons is *chao shou*, which means "crossed hands," as the wontons are folded in such a way that the tips cross each other like arms. This is one of my favorite Sichuan dishes of all time, with a deliciously savory, tangy, garlicky, and spicy sauce that is positively addictive. In the words of a student who recently attended one of my dumpling classes, the sauce "is so good I can just drink it straight."

WONTONS

8 dried shiitake mushrooms

1 pound ground pork

5 scallions, thinly sliced, plus more (optional) for garnish

1 tablespoon soy sauce

1 tablespoon Chinese rice wine or dry sherry

1 tablespoon sesame oil

One 1-pound package wonton wrappers

SAUCE

2 cloves garlic, minced

1/4 cup soy sauce

1/2 tablespoon sugar

3 tablespoons Sichuan chili oil

2 tablespoons Chinese black vinegar or good-quality balsamic vinegar

1. Make the wontons: Soak the shiitake mushrooms in warm water until fully softened, 15 to 20 minutes. Drain, squeeze out the excess water, discard the stems, and finely chop the caps.

2. In a large bowl, mix together the chopped shiitake mushrooms, ground pork, scallions, soy sauce, rice wine, and sesame oil.

3. Keep the extra wrappers covered with a barely damp towel until ready to use, to prevent them from drying out. Have a small dish of water on hand for sealing the wontons.

4. Angle a wonton wrapper so that it faces you like a diamond. Place 1 heaping teaspoon of filling in the center of the wrapper (see a). Add water along the 4 edges with your fingertips. Form a triangle by folding the bottom tip up to the top tip and pinching out as much air as possible. Seal the sides (see b). With a long side of the triangle facing you, dab a bit of water on the tip of the left side, and fold it over the right (see c).

RECIPE CONTINUES

5. Place the finished wontons on a plate and covered with a barely damp kitchen towel while you repeat to make more wontons.

6. Prepare the sauce: In a medium bowl, mix together the garlic, soy sauce, sugar, Sichuan chili oil, and black vinegar. Stir until the sugar is fully dissolved and set aside.

7. Bring a large pot of water to a boil. Working in batches, boil the wontons until they float to the top, 4 to 5 minutes. Remove them with a wire-mesh skimmer or slotted spoon and transfer to a serving dish. Coat the wontons with the sauce, garnish with the extra scallions (if using), and serve.

TIP

Any wontons you don't cook right away can be frozen. Line a small plate or tray with parchment paper, and place the wontons on the parchment in a single layer (they can touch but they shouldn't be on top of one another). Freeze the wontons for 2 hours until they are fully frozen, and then you can transfer them to a freezer bag or other storage container. This way, they pull apart very easily when you're ready to cook. And there's no need to defrost before cooking; you can cook them straight out of the freezer and just add 1 minute more to the boiling time.

SICHUAN CHILI OIL

SICHUAN-STYLE PEANUT NOODLES

SERVES 4 TO 6 Whenever I teach Sichuan cooking classes, at least one or two students ask me about the cold noodles tossed with a spicy peanut sauce served at their local Sichuan takeout. "How do we make those?" they wonder. In reality, the Sichuan peanut noodles most Americans know are actually Western riffs on dan dan noodles, traditional spicy noodles topped with a thick, sesame pork sauce. Although born out of American Chinese restaurants, these New World Sichuan-style peanut noodles are no less hearty and delicious. This is my vegetarian version, noodles coated with a tingly peanut sauce infused with Sichuan chili oil. They are so addictive I've never had any leftovers.

½ pound baby bok choy

10 ounces dried thick wheat noodles, or 16 ounces fresh noodles

2 tablespoons sesame oil

2 tablespoons vegetable oil

2 teaspoons minced garlic

2 teaspoons minced or grated fresh ginger

8 fresh shiitake mushrooms, stems discarded and caps thinly sliced

½ cup smooth peanut butter

¼ cup Sichuan chili oil

¼ cup soy sauce

¼ cup Chinese black vinegar

1 tablespoon sugar

1 teaspoon crushed red chili flakes

1 teaspoon ground Sichuan pepper

1 cucumber, peeled and julienned

2 teaspoons toasted white sesame seeds

2 scallions, finely chopped

1. Trim the rough ends off the baby bok choy. Separate the leaves, rinse under cold water to remove any dirt, and dry with clean kitchen towels. Cut into thin, bite-size pieces.

2. Bring a pot of water to a boil and cook the noodles for the minimum amount of time according to the package instructions. Drain immediately, rinse with cold water, and drain again. Return the noodles to the pot or transfer to a mixing bowl. Toss with the sesame oil until well coated and set aside.

3. In a large skillet, heat the vegetable oil over medium heat. Add the garlic and ginger and cook until just fragrant, 30 to 40 seconds. Remove the toasted garlic and ginger from the pan and set aside. Add the mushrooms to the pan and cook until they begin to turn golden, 1 to 2 minutes. Add the bok choy and cook for 30 seconds; they should be lightly cooked but still retain a crisp snap.

4. In a medium bowl, whisk together the peanut butter and 2 tablespoons water until smooth. Whisk in the Sichuan chili oil, soy sauce, black vinegar, sugar, chili flakes, and Sichuan pepper. Stir in the toasted garlic and ginger.

5. Pour the sauce over the noodles and toss thoroughly, making sure all the noodles are well coated. Transfer to a large bowl or deep serving dish and add the cucumber and mushroom/bok choy mixture on top. Sprinkle with the sesame seeds and scallions. Toss before dividing into individual bowls.

RED-COOKED BEEF WITH DAIKON RADISH

SERVES 6 AS PART OF A MULTICOURSE MEAL This Chinese beef stew—made b
marbled beef in a combination of soy sauce, cinnamon, star anise, tangerin
as aromatic and delicious as it sounds. Be sure to use beef that still contain
marbling; the meat will become meltingly tender after 90 minutes of slow, g
daikon radish, which should be cut into large pieces, will also become tende
sponge for the sauce. Like other braised dishes, it gets better after sitting ov
have a chance to develop more. So don't be afraid to make this ahead of tim
rice on hand, whether for a dinner party or a weeknight meal.

3 tablespoons peanut oil or
vegetable oil

2 pounds beef short ribs, or
1 pound beef chuck or stew
meat cut into 2-inch pieces

½ cup all-purpose flour

1 large yellow onion, diced

2 tablespoons Chinese rice
wine or dry sherry

3 tablespoons soy sauce

2 tablespoons sugar

One 1-inch piece fresh ginger,
peeled and cut into 3 pieces

2 cloves garlic, minced

1 cinnamon stick

2 whole star anise

2 pieces dried tangerine peel

3 tab
2 tab
chi
1 pou
and
the
Salt a
pep
Rice, f

1. In a large heavy-bottomed pot, Dutch oven, or wok, heat 2 tablespoons of the oil over medium-high heat.

2. Using tongs, toss the beef lightly in the flour in a shallow dish. Add the beef to the pan and sear until lightly browned all around, about 2 minutes. Transfer the beef to a plate and set aside.

3. Reduce the heat to medium. In the same pot, heat the remaining 1 tablespoon oil. Add the onion and sauté until aromatic and softened, 2 to 3 minutes. Return the beef to the pot. Add the rice wine and stir to lift any beef drippings

from the bottom of t
water, the soy sauce,
garlic, cinnamon, sta
peel, Sichuan chili oi
Bring the liquid to a
to a gentle simmer. C
50 minutes, stirring c

4. Add the daikon to the
tender and the sauce
enough to coat the ba
another 30 to 40 minu
and adjust the season
black pepper if neede
large serving dish and
rice.

MAPO TOFU RAMEN (MABO RAMEN)

SERVES 4 AS PART OF A MULTICOURSE MEAL, OR 2 AS A MAIN DISH Years ago, while in Japan for the first time, I took a day trip from Tokyo to Yokohama, which was only about half an hour away by train. The city boasts the largest Chinatown in Japan with alleyways reminiscent of Beijing's older neighborhoods. It was in one of these alleys that I found a ramen shop, where the special of the day was the mapo tofu ramen. The bowl of ramen arrived bright red and still bubbling, with a thick and spicy sauce that maintained the textural integrity of Sichuan mapo tofu, and it was fiery enough to be true to the Chinese original.

Back home, I experimented with this Chinese-Japanese hybrid dish to come up with a version closest to that glorious bowl I had in Yokohama. Mapo tofu is traditionally made with *doubanjiang,* a Chinese fermented chili paste that must be made outdoors in large earthenware containers; I buy it in Chinese markets, but you can also substitute Korean gochujang, which has a similar earthy and spicy flavor profile.

½ pound ground pork or beef

3 tablespoons Chinese rice
wine or dry sherry

2 tablespoons fermented
black beans

2 tablespoons Sichuan chili oil

2 tablespoons doubanjiang
(Chinese chili bean paste)
or gochujang

2 teaspoons soy sauce

1 teaspoon sesame oil

1 teaspoon sugar

½ teaspoon ground Sichuan
pepper

½ teaspoon cayenne pepper

1 tablespoon peanut oil or
vegetable oil

2 scallions, chopped, white
and green parts kept
separate

1 clove garlic, minced

1 teaspoon minced fresh
ginger

3 cups chicken stock

½ block soft or medium-firm
tofu (about ½ pound),
drained and cut into 1-inch
cubes

3 tablespoons cornstarch

Salt

8 ounces fresh ramen, or two
3-ounce packages instant
ramen

1. In a large bowl, combine the pork and Chinese rice wine and break it apart as much as possible with a large spoon. Set aside to marinate for 10 minutes.

2. In a small bowl, mash the fermented black beans with the back of a spoon for 20 seconds. Stir in the Sichuan chili oil, doubanjiang, soy sauce, sesame oil, sugar, Sichuan pepper, and cayenne. Set the black bean mixture aside.

RECIPE CONTINUES

3. Heat a wok or large skillet over high heat until a bead of water sizzles and evaporates on contact. Add the oil and swirl to coat the bottom. Add the pork and stir-fry, breaking up the meat with a spatula, until no longer pink, about 2 minutes. Reduce the heat to medium, then add the scallion whites, garlic, and ginger. Stir-fry briefly until fragrant, about 30 seconds.

4. Add the black bean mixture and chicken stock. Bring the liquid to a boil, then reduce to a simmer. Add the tofu cubes. Dissolve the cornstarch in ¼ cup water and stir into the broth. Allow the broth to thicken and simmer for another 5 minutes. Season with salt to taste.

5. Meanwhile, bring boil and cook the package instructi the ramen into in

6. Season the mapo salt if needed. Lad over the ramen an scallion greens.

BON BON CHICKEN (COLD CHICKEN WITH CUCUMBERS IN SESAME SAUCE)

SERVES 4 AS AN APPETIZER OR SIDE DISH This Sichuan dish, also called Bang Bang Chicken, is named for the sounds of the traditional way of tenderizing chicken for this dish, by hitting it with a stick or hammer. My easier preparation involves using cold leftover roast chicken, preferably dark meat or a mix of dark and white meat. The only hitting sounds involve grinding the garlic into a paste with a mortar and pestle. The chicken and cucumbers are tossed in a garlicky, hot, and numbing sesame sauce. It's the ultimate refreshing appetizer for a warm evening.

1 tablespoon white sesame
   seeds

4 Kirby cucumbers, or
   2 regular cucumbers

5 cloves garlic

1 teaspoon salt

1 teaspoon grated fresh ginger

1/3 cup tahini

1/3 cup Sichuan chili oil

2 tablespoons soy sauce

2 tablespoons Chinese black
   vinegar or good-quality
   balsamic vinegar

1 teaspoon sesame oil

1/2 tablespoon sugar

1/2 teaspoon ground Sichuan
   pepper

3/4 pound cold roast chicken,
   shredded and rewarmed

2 scallions, thinly sliced

1. In a small dry skillet, toast the sesame seeds until they become lightly browned and aromatic, about 1 minute. Transfer to a dish and set aside.

2. Peel the cucumber(s) and quarter lengthwise. Scoop out the middle part with seeds. Cut the remainder of the cucumber(s) into matchsticks, then transfer to a plate.

3. Smash and peel the garlic cloves and place in a mortar with the salt. Mash the garlic until it resembles a thick paste (the salt not only enhances the flavor of the garlic but also draws out its juices during mashing). If you don't have a mortar and pestle, pulse the garlic and salt in a food processor until you have a thick paste.

4. In a large bowl, combine the mashed garlic paste, ginger, tahini, Sichuan chili oil, soy sauce, black vinegar, sesame oil, sugar, and Sichuan pepper. Whisk until smooth.

5. In a large bowl, toss the shredded chicken and cucumbers with the sauce. Sprinkle the toasted sesame seeds and scallions on top and serve.

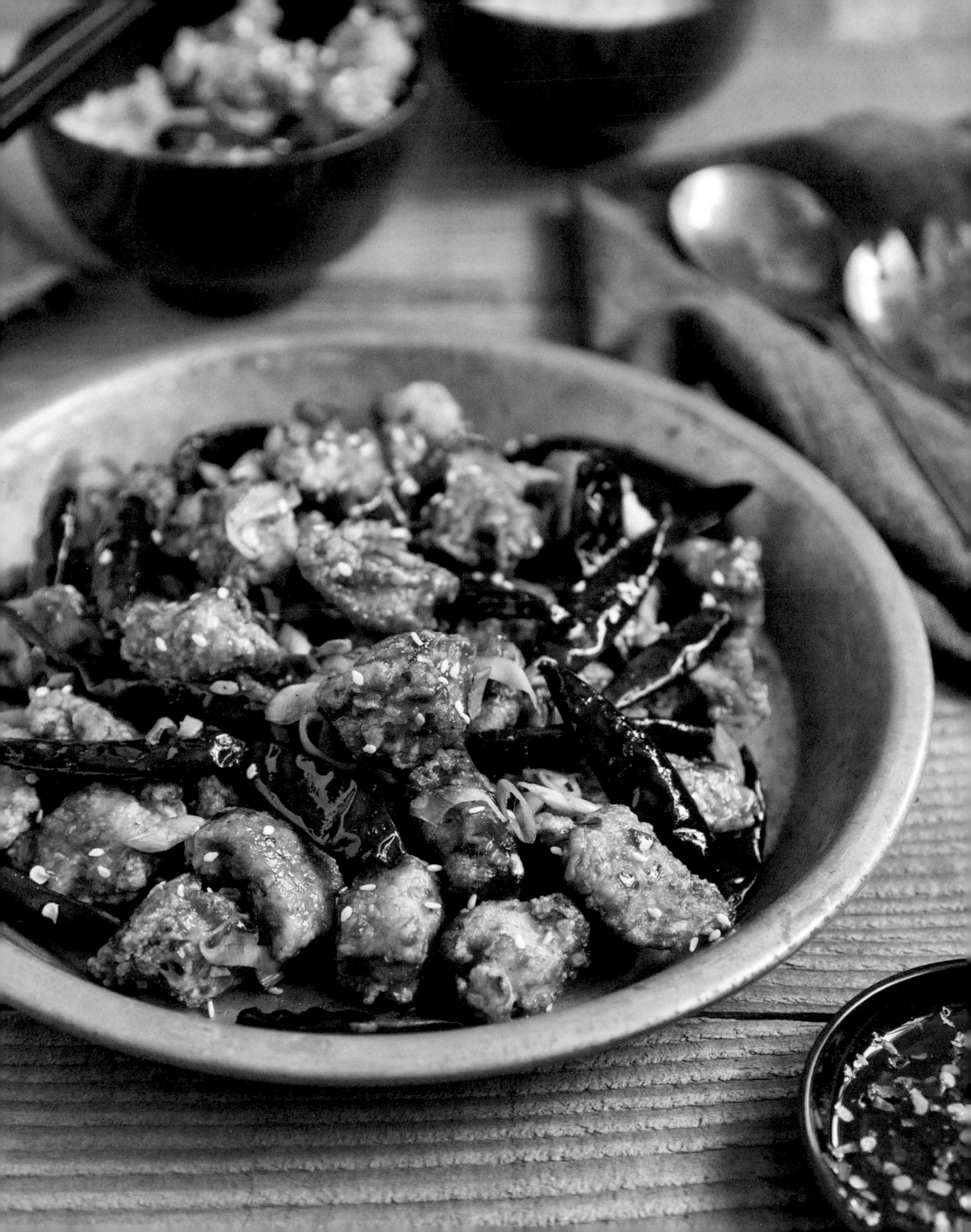

CHONGQING CHICKEN (LA ZI JI)

SERVES 4 Anyone who has spent enough time in good Sichuan restaurants is bound to eventually see a dish called Chongqing Chicken, or *la zi ji* in Mandarin. A classic Sichuan favorite, the dish consists of small nuggets of golden fried chicken heaped with bright-red, smoky dried chilies. It's the perfect entree for anyone who loves crispy textures and hot flavors. Instead of deep-frying, I use a double shallow-frying method that allows the chicken to crisp up without using a ton of oil. Few fried chicken entrees are enveloped by such a succulent tongue-tingling sauce.

MARINADE AND CHICKEN

2 tablespoons soy sauce

2 tablespoons Chinese rice wine or dry sherry

2 egg whites

1 pound chicken breast, cut into 1-inch cubes

SAUCE

3 tablespoons Sichuan chili oil

1 tablespoon soy sauce

1 tablespoon chicken stock or water

1 teaspoon Chinese black vinegar or good-quality balsamic vinegar

1 teaspoon cornstarch

1 teaspoon ground Sichuan pepper

FOR FRYING THE CHICKEN

1½ cups cornstarch

2 teaspoons salt

1 teaspoon freshly ground black pepper

3 cups plus 1 tablespoon peanut oil or vegetable oil

15 dried red chilies (such as Tien Tsin, Japonés, or Thai spur chilies)

1 leek, white part only, thinly sliced

3 cloves garlic, minced

1 teaspoon minced fresh ginger

1 scallion, thinly sliced

1. Marinate the chicken: In a large bowl, combine the soy sauce, rice wine, and egg whites. Add the chicken, toss to coat with the marinade mixture, and let sit for 10 minutes.

2. Make the sauce: In a bowl, mix together the Sichuan chili oil, soy sauce, chicken stock, Chinese black vinegar, cornstarch, and Sichuan pepper. Set the sauce aside.

3. To fry the chicken: In a large bowl or plate, mix together the cornstarch, salt, and black pepper. Dredge the chicken in the cornstarch mixture and shake off the excess cornstarch.

4. Pour 3 cups of the peanut oil into a wok and heat until the temperature reads 350°F on a deep-fry thermometer. Working in two or three batches, add the chicken cubes and fry until golden brown on the outside and cooked

RECIPE CONTINUES

through, 4 to 5 minutes, carefully flipping the pieces with tongs to cook evenly. Transfer the chicken to a plate lined with paper towels to drain.

5. Pour the oil out of the wok into a heatproof container and save for discarding. Wipe the wok with a paper towel to remove any browned bits, but don't wash.

6. Reheat the wok over medium-high heat. Add the remaining 1 tablespoon oil and swirl to coat the bottom. Add the dried chilies to the wok and stir-fry just until fragrant, 20 to 30 seconds. Add the leek, garlic, and ginger and stir-fry until the leek has softened, 1 to 2 minutes. Stir in the sauce mixture and simmer until slightly thickened, about 1 minute. Add the fried chicken, toss to combine, and remove from the heat. Sprinkle the scallions on top and serve immediately.

TAME THE FLAMES

Even the most ardent chili-heads may need to cool a burning mouth when feasting on an especially hot meal. While beer and soda may be refreshing for moderately spiced food (see What Do You Sip with Spicy Food?, page 207), carbonation actually spreads the capsaicin around in your mouth, accentuating the heat of intensely spicy dishes. And water may not help either when your mouth is on fire. To get scientific, capsaicin has nonpolar molecules, which can only dissolve with other nonpolar molecules. Water is only made with polar molecules and won't provide relief even in iced form; in fact, it can spread the burning sensation.

Instead, when you feel your mouth on fire, have some milk nearby for quick relief. Milk and milk products contain both nonpolar molecules and casein proteins, which neutralize the capsaicin. It's why many Indian dishes contain yogurt. And don't fret if you're not a fan of milk; capsaicin also dissolves in high-fat foods such as coconut. Plain coconut water or coconut milk can work miracles, or for a thicker and creamier drink, try an Avocado Coconut Shake (page 233).

HOT AND SOUR CABBAGE

SERVES 4 AS PART OF A MULTICOURSE MEAL In many parts of China, especially the northern regions, cabbage is one of the only vegetables widely available in the winter. There are many different ways to prepare it that range from braising to pickling to stir-frying. This hot and sour stir-fry may appear simple, but has a pretty complex flavor profile that is equally spicy, tangy, sweet, and sour. It's a great quick side dish to add to your multicourse meal.

1 pound napa cabbage leaves

2 tablespoons Sichuan chili oil

1 tablespoon soy sauce

1 tablespoon Chinese black vinegar or good-quality balsamic vinegar

1 tablespoon light brown sugar

2 tablespoons vegetable oil

8 dried red chilies (such as Tien Tsin, Japonés, or Thai spur chilies), stems removed

3 cloves garlic, minced

1/2 tablespoon grated fresh ginger

Salt

1. Cut the rough ends off the napa cabbage leaves. Cut the leaves into about 1½-inch squares.

2. In a small bowl, stir together the Sichuan chili oil, soy sauce, black vinegar, and brown sugar. Set the chili oil mixture aside.

3. Heat a wok or large skillet over high heat until a bead of water sizzles and evaporates on contact. Add the vegetable oil and swirl to coat the bottom. Add the dried red chilies and stir-fry until they start to to blacken, about 30 seconds. Add the garlic and ginger and stir-fry just until aromatic, about 30 seconds. Add the cabbage and stir-fry until softened and lightly charred in spots, about 5 minutes. Pour in the chili oil mixture and cook, tossing, until the liquid is absorbed, 1 to 2 minutes. Adjust the seasoning with salt if needed. Transfer to a plate and serve.

SICHUAN CUCUMBER AND RADISH SALAD

SERVES 4 TO 6 AS AN APPETIZER OR SIDE DISH Fans of Sichuan cuisine know that even spice fiends need something to ward off all the heat in your mouth between bites. Cucumber salads are served at almost every Sichuan restaurant I've been to, and are good appetizers as well as good palate cleansers between the spicier dishes served as part of a multicourse meal. I recommend making this salad the day before you plan on serving it (and keep it refrigerated) so the flavors have time to develop and deepen, but you'll still notice a big difference when you taste it 30 minutes after mixing.

4 Kirby cucumbers, washed and unpeeled

1/2 pound red radishes

1 teaspoon salt

1/2 tablespoon peanut oil or vegetable oil

1 tablespoon minced garlic

2 tablespoons Sichuan chili oil

1 tablespoon rice vinegar

1 teaspoon soy sauce

1 teaspoon sesame oil

1 teaspoon sugar

1/4 teaspoon ground Sichuan pepper

1. Halve the cucumbers lengthwise, then cut each in half again so you have quartered strips. Cut or scoop out the seedy middle section. Slice each strip crosswise into 1½-inch lengths.

2. Trim the radishes and cut into thin slices. Combine the radishes and cucumbers in a large bowl and toss with the salt. Let sit for 5 minutes.

3. Heat a small skillet over medium-low heat. Add the peanut oil, then add the garlic and cook until fragrant, about 1 minute, being careful to not let the garlic burn. Transfer to a small bowl and stir in the Sichuan chili oil, rice vinegar, soy sauce, sesame oil, sugar, and Sichuan pepper.

4. Toss the cucumbers and radishes with the rice vinegar mixture. Transfer to a serving dish and serve at room temperature, or chill in the fridge until ready to serve. The salad will keep for up to 4 days in the fridge.

KUNG PAO SWEET POTATOES

SERVES 4 Many people think that in Chinese cooking, in order to have a vegetarian main course, you need to use tofu, seitan, or another protein substitute. And so many Chinese restaurants do, it seems like an easy default. But sometimes it's nice to get a little creative with your ingredients. I love making kung pao sweet potatoes, a rift on kung pao chicken, for a Sichuan meal with vegetarian friends. Sweet potatoes are filling and nutrient-packed enough to be the star of a main dish, and, when cut into small pieces, take only 8 minutes to cook when you stir-fry them in a wok, no parboiling necessary.

1 tablespoon Chinese black vinegar or good-quality balsamic vinegar

1 tablespoon soy sauce

2 teaspoons hoisin sauce

2 teaspoons Sichuan chili oil

1 teaspoon sesame oil

1 tablespoon sugar

1 teaspoon ground Sichuan pepper

3 tablespoons vegetable oil

8 to 10 dried red chilies (such as Tien Tsin, Japonés, or Thai spur chilies)

1 pound sweet potatoes, peeled and cut into 1-inch cubes

5 scallions, thinly sliced, white and green parts kept separate

2 cloves garlic, minced

1 teaspoon minced or grated fresh ginger

1/4 cup unsalted dry-roasted peanuts or cashews

1. In a small bowl, combine the vinegar, soy sauce, hoisin sauce, Sichuan chili oil, sesame oil, sugar, and Sichuan pepper. Stir until the sugar is dissolved. Set the sauce aside.

2. You may need to turn on your stove's exhaust fan, because stir-frying dried chilies on high heat can get a little smoky. Heat a wok or large skillet over high heat until a bead of water sizzles and evaporates on contact. Add 2 tablespoons of the vegetable oil and swirl to coat the bottom. Add the chilies and stir-fry until the chilies have just begun to blacken and the oil is slightly fragrant, about 30 seconds. Add the sweet potatoes and stir-fry until the outsides are golden brown and the sweet potato is starting to soften, 7 to 8 minutes.

3. By now the pan will be a little dry. Create a well in the middle of the pan and pour in the remaining 1 tablespoon vegetable oil. Add the scallion whites, garlic, and ginger and stir-fry for 30 seconds. Pour in the sauce and mix to coat the other ingredients. Simmer the mixture for 1 to 2 minutes to thicken. Stir in the peanuts and cook for another minute. Transfer to a serving plate, sprinkle the scallion greens on top, and serve.

SMOKY STIR-FRIED TOFU WITH GARLIC CHIVES AND YELLOW SQUASH

SERVES 4 AS PART OF A MULTICOURSE MEAL Available at many Chinese and Korean grocery stores, garlic chives have mild garlic and onion flavors that make them excellent for stir-fries. If you don't have garlic chives, use garlic scapes or scallions as a substitute.

1 tablespoon vegetable oil

8 dried red chilies (such as Tien Tsin, Japonés, or Thai spur chilies)

1 teaspoon minced fresh ginger

8 ounces smoked or baked tofu, cut into bite-size pieces about 1/4 inch thick

1 small yellow squash, cut into bite-size pieces about 1/2 inch thick

2 tablespoons Chinese rice wine or dry sherry

4 ounces Chinese garlic chives, cut into 3-inch lengths

2 to 3 tablespoons Sichuan chili oil

Salt and freshly ground white pepper

Heat a wok or large skillet over high heat until a drop of water sizzles and evaporates on contact. Add the vegetable oil and swirl to coat the bottom. Add the dried chilies and ginger and stir-fry until fragrant, about 20 seconds. Add the tofu and stir-fry for about 1 minute. Add the yellow squash and rice wine and cook until slightly softened, about 1 minute. Add the garlic chives and Sichuan chili oil and stir-fry for another minute. Season to taste with salt and white pepper. Transfer to a plate and serve.

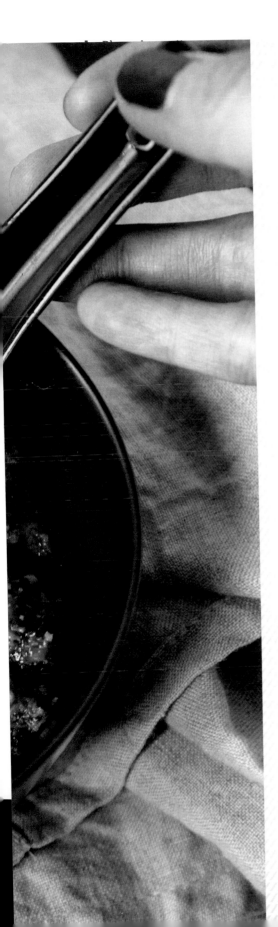

XO SAUCE

BAKED FLATBREAD "PIZZA" WITH XO SAUCE, MUSHROOMS, AND SHAVED BRUSSELS SPROUTS

MAKES 4 INDIVIDUAL FLATBREAD PIZZAS As a small apartment dweller and the owner of a small oven, I don't have room in my kitchen for a pizza stone. When I get a pizza craving, I head to a market to pick up flatbread or pitas, which toast up easily no matter what size oven you have. This is an unconventional take on flatbread pizza, but once you taste how amazingly the XO sauce pairs with shallots, mushrooms, and crispy Brussels sprouts, this spicy snack or light meal just might go on heavy rotation.

6 ounces Brussels sprouts

6 tablespoons olive oil

10 fresh shiitake or cremini mushrooms, stems discarded and caps thinly sliced

2 large shallots, thinly sliced

4 store-bought flatbreads or pitas about 6 inches in diameter

1 cup XO sauce

1/2 teaspoon flaky sea salt

1. Preheat the oven to 450°F. Line a baking sheet with foil or parchment paper.

2. Lay each Brussels sprout on its side on a cutting board, hold it steady by the stem end, and cut into very thin slices with a chef's knife. Use your hands to separate the layers in a bowl and toss with 1 tablespoon of the olive oil.

3. In another bowl, toss the mushrooms and shallots with another 1 tablespoon of the olive oil and set aside.

4. Arrange the flatbreads on the lined baking sheet. Brush the tops and sides of the bread with the remaining 3 tablespoons olive oil (you might not need the full 3 tablespoons). Spread the XO sauce evenly over each bread, leaving a 1/2-inch border all around without sauce. Scatter the shallot/mushroom mixture over the sauce, then scatter the Brussels sprouts on top. Sprinkle the sea salt over the Brussels sprouts.

5. Bake until the edges of the flatbread are golden and the Brussels sprouts are becoming crispy, 10 to 12 minutes. Carefully remove from the oven, slice into quarters, and serve.

XO SAUCE CASHEW CHICKEN

SERVES 4 AS PART OF A MULTICOURSE MEAL, OR 2 AS A MAIN DISH You can easily use XO sauce to spice up your favorite humble stir-fry. I thought Chinese cashew chicken was already perfect on its own, but one night decided to add a few spoonfuls of XO sauce that was sitting in the fridge. And wow, what a revelation! Mixed with a few other simple ingredients, the XO sauce takes this Chinese takeout classic to a new level.

1 tablespoon Chinese rice wine or dry sherry

1 tablespoon cornstarch

1 pound boneless, skinless chicken breast, cut into 1-inch cubes

3 tablespoons XO sauce

2 tablespoons soy sauce

1 teaspoon hoisin sauce

1 teaspoon sesame oil

1 teaspoon crushed red chili flakes

2 tablespoons peanut oil or vegetable oil

1 medium yellow onion, diced

1 red bell pepper, diced

2 cloves garlic, finely chopped

1/2 cup unsalted roasted cashews

1. In a small bowl, stir together the rice wine and cornstarch until the cornstarch is fully dissolved. Place the chicken in a large bowl, pour the marinade over the chicken, and stir until the chicken is evenly covered. Let sit at room temperature for 10 minutes.

2. In a small bowl, mix together the XO sauce, soy sauce, hoisin sauce, sesame oil, and chili flakes. Set the XO sauce mixture aside.

3. Heat a wok or large skillet over medium-high heat until a bead of water sizzles and evaporates on contact. Add the peanut oil and swirl to coat the bottom. Add the marinated chicken and stir-fry just until no longer pink on the outside, about 2 minutes.

4. Add the onion, bell pepper, and garlic and stir-fry until fragrant and the onion starts to become translucent, 2 to 3 minutes.

5. Add the XO sauce mixture and stir to coat the chicken. Stir-fry for another 1 to 2 minutes to allow the chicken to cook through (if you're unsure, cut a piece open to check for doneness), then stir in the cashews. Transfer to a plate and serve.

STIR-FRIED RICE CAKES WITH ZUCCHINI, MUSHROOMS, AND XO SAUCE

SERVES 4 AS PART OF A MULTICOURSE MEAL I often crave the chewy texture of rice cakes, also known as *nian gao* in Mandarin. You can find fresh rice cakes in Chinese or Korean grocery stores, usually in the refrigerated section near the fresh noodles and tofu. They will need to soak in room-temperature water for 2 hours (or more depending on package instructions). Or you can use frozen rice cakes, which you have to thaw before soaking. Stir-fried with XO sauce and vegetables, they are an addictive entree alongside other dishes at the table, or just eaten on their own.

8 ounces fresh rice cakes

3 tablespoons vegetable oil

2 cloves garlic, minced

1 teaspoon minced fresh ginger

1 shallot, thinly sliced

1 large zucchini, cut into half-moons about 1/2 inch thick

12 fresh shiitake mushrooms, stems discarded and caps thinly sliced

1/3 cup chicken stock or vegetable broth

2 tablespoons Chinese rice wine or dry sherry

2 cups shredded cabbage

1/4 cup XO sauce

1 teaspoon rice vinegar

Salt

1. Soak the rice cakes in room-temperature water for 2 hours or according to package directions. Drain.

2. Heat a wok or large skillet over medium-high heat until a bead of water sizzles and evaporates on contact. Add 2 tablespoons of the vegetable oil and swirl to coat the bottom. Add the garlic, ginger, and shallot and stir-fry just until aromatic, about 20 seconds. Add the zucchini and shiitake mushrooms and cook for 1 minute.

3. Add the remaining 1 tablespoon oil and the rice cakes and stir-fry until they start to turn golden, about 2 minutes. Add the stock or broth, cover the wok or skillet with a lid, and let steam until the rice cakes have softened and most of the liquid is gone, 2 to 3 minutes. Uncover and add the rice wine, scraping the bottom of the pan with a spatula if any of the rice cakes have gotten stuck to the bottom. Add the cabbage, XO sauce, and rice vinegar. Stir so that everything in the pan gets evenly coated and cook for another minute. Adjust the seasoning with salt if needed. Transfer to a plate and serve.

XO SAUCE DRY-FRIED GREEN BEANS

SERVES 4 AS A SIDE DISH Dry-frying is a method of cooking a vegetable or protein with minimal sauces for a longer period of time than stir-frying in order to wring out the moisture. The technique creates a crispier or chewier dish. I borrowed this method from Sichuan dry-fried green beans, a classic and delectable dish of crisp yet tender beans flavored with dried chilies and Sichuan pepper. Here, the beans are fried in more oil than you would use for a stir-fry and briskly stirred with a spatula, to develop the characteristic wrinkled and blistered surface. The XO sauce lends a wonderful smokiness and deep caramelized flavor to the green beans.

3/4 pound green beans

1 tablespoon Chinese rice wine or dry sherry

3 tablespoons XO sauce

1 teaspoon crushed red chili flakes

1/2 teaspoon sugar

1/4 cup peanut oil or vegetable oil

8 dried red chilies (such as Tien Tsin, Japonés, or Thai spur chilies)

1 shallot, finely chopped

Salt

1. Rinse the green beans and dry them thoroughly (even a small amount of water will cause oil in the wok to spit). Cut the beans into 2-inch lengths.

2. In a small bowl, stir together the rice wine, XO sauce, chili flakes, and sugar until the sugar is dissolved. Set the sauce aside.

3. Heat a wok or large skillet over high heat until a bead of water sizzles and evaporates on contact. Add the peanut oil and swirl to coat the bottom. Add the green beans and stir-fry, keeping the beans constantly moving, until they begin to blister and wilt, 5 to 6 minutes.

4. Add the chilies and shallot and stir-fry until fragrant, about 30 seconds. Add the sauce and stir to coat the green beans evenly. Season with salt if needed. Transfer to a plate and serve hot.

ENOKI MUSHROOMS WITH XO GARLIC SAUCE

SERVES 4 AS A SIDE DISH Enoki mushrooms are another quick-cooking vegetable that pairs well with XO sauce for a side dish. In this method, you simply bring water to a boil in a wok or a pot wide enough to fit a wire-mesh colander, and cook the mushrooms for about 2 minutes. Cooking them in the colander will make them easy to drain and transfer to the serving dish when they're done. Adding crisp garlic and ginger to the XO sauce will make it extra aromatic.

12 ounces enoki mushrooms

1/4 cup XO sauce

3 tablespoons soy sauce

3 tablespoons mirin

1 tablespoon sesame oil

2 teaspoons vegetable oil

5 cloves garlic, minced

1 teaspoon grated fresh ginger

2 scallions, thinly sliced, white and green parts kept separate

1. Trim off 1 to 2 inches of the root section of the enoki mushrooms until you can easily pull apart the strands with your fingers. Separate the strands and rinse in a colander to clean.

2. In a small bowl, combine the XO sauce, soy sauce, mirin, and sesame oil.

3. Fill a wok about halfway with water. Bring the water to a boil. Working in 2 batches, place the enoki mushrooms in a wire-mesh colander and submerge the bottom of the colander in the boiling water. Cook the enoki mushrooms in the colander for 2 minutes, using tongs to hold down the mushrooms if they start to float. Lift the colander from the water, drain off the excess water, and use the tongs to transfer the mushrooms to a serving dish.

4. Heat a small saucepan over medium heat. Add the vegetable oil and swirl to coat the bottom. Add the garlic, ginger, and scallion whites and cook just until aromatic, about 20 seconds. Add the XO sauce mixture, bring to a simmer, and simmer for 30 seconds. Remove from the heat and stir in the scallion greens. Spoon the sauce over the enoki mushrooms and serve.

GOCHUJANG

KIMCHI

MAKES 2¼ TO 3 CUPS If you're a kimchi fiend like I am, and put it on everything from scrambled eggs to noodle soups, making your own kimchi at home is much more economical than buying multiple jars a month. It's also much simpler than many people would think. You'll need to first weigh the cabbage leaves down overnight to wring out excess water, but after that the steps for mixing the flavoring and fermenting the kimchi are incredibly easy. To get the napa cabbage leaves coated evenly, be sure to don some gloves and mix the leaves thoroughly with your hands.

2 pounds napa cabbage

2 tablespoons coarse sea salt

3 tablespoons gochujang

2 tablespoons gochugaru

2 teaspoons minced garlic

1 teaspoon grated fresh ginger

2 teaspoons sugar

1. Remove the outer leaves and the core from the cabbage. Separate the inner leaves, rinse them well under cold water, and shake off any excess water. Cut the leaves into 2-inch squares and toss with the salt in a large nonreactive bowl. Place a bowl or another heavy-ish object on top of the cabbage to weigh down the leaves and leave alone for 12 hours.

2. In a small bowl, whisk together the gochujang, gochugaru, garlic, ginger, and sugar.

3. Squeeze the excess water from the cabbage and return to the large bowl. Add the gochujang mixture and use your hands to thoroughly mix it with the cabbage. Transfer the cabbage to a jar and tightly pack the leaves in. Let stand at room temperature for 48 hours with the lid loosely on (fermentation will build up a lot of pressure in the jar), then chill in the fridge for 3 days before serving. The kimchi will last for 6 months in the fridge.

FRESH CUCUMBER KIMCHI

SERVES 4 Cucumber kimchi is a popular *banchan* (small side dish) in Korea all year round, but especially in the summer, when cucumbers are in season. This is called a quick kimchi or fresh kimchi because it doesn't need to ferment. You'll want to take out the seeds to help the cucumbers stay crunchy, but then just toss them with the garlicky gochujang sauce for a crunchy, refreshing snack or side dish.

1 pound Kirby cucumbers	1 tablespoon gochujang	1 teaspoon sugar
1 teaspoon salt	1 teaspoon sesame oil	2 cloves garlic, minced
1½ tablespoons rice vinegar	1 teaspoon gochugaru	2 teaspoons sesame seeds

1. Quarter the cucumbers lengthwise and cut or scrape out the seeds (this helps the cucumber stay crunchy). Cut the lengths into bite-size pieces. Transfer to a large bowl and toss with the salt.

2. In a small bowl, whisk together the rice vinegar, gochujang, sesame oil, gochugaru, sugar, and garlic until the sugar is dissolved. Pour the gochujang mixture over the cucumbers, add the sesame seeds, and toss thoroughly. Let stand at room temperature or chill for at least 30 minutes before serving to deepen the flavors. The cucumbers will keep refrigerated for up to 1 week.

VEGETARIAN BIBIMBAP WITH BROWN RICE

SERVES 2 AS A MAIN DISH Bibimbap is an ideal one-bowl comfort food dish, as perfect for breakfast as it is for a 2 a.m. meal after bar hopping. It's pure delight to pour the hot gochujang-based sauce over all the vegetables, eggs, and rice and mix everything until it looks like a sublime mess. And you can make bibimbap whether or not you own a *dolsot* (stone bowl). The instructions below provide three options for the rice: making sizzling bibimbap rice in a dolsot, a simple alternative crispy rice involving wok or skillet, or going the minimalist route with steamed rice.

1½ cups brown rice

2 tablespoons gochujang

1 tablespoon rice vinegar

2 teaspoons honey

1 teaspoon plus
   1½ tablespoons sesame oil

12 ounces baby spinach

1 teaspoon toasted white
   sesame seeds

3 tablespoons vegetable oil,
   plus more for the crispy rice
   (step 6)

2 large eggs

8 fresh shiitake mushrooms,
   stems discarded and caps
   thinly sliced

2 teaspoons soy sauce

1 Persian (mini) or other
   seedless cucumber,
   very thinly sliced

1 medium carrot, julienned

1 cup soybean sprouts

½ cup kimchi

1. In a small saucepan, combine the brown rice and 4½ cups water. Bring to a simmer over medium heat, 3 to 5 minutes. Reduce the heat to low, cover, and cook until the water is fully absorbed, 30 to 40 minutes. Remove from the heat, fluff the grains with a rice spatula, and keep covered until the other ingredients are ready.

2. In a small bowl, whisk together the gochujang, 1 tablespoon water, the vinegar, honey, and 1 teaspoon of the sesame oil until smooth. Set the bibimbap sauce aside.

3. Bring a medium pot of water to a boil. Add the spinach and cook just until the leaves are softened but still bright green, about 30 seconds. Drain, rinse under cold water, and squeeze out the excess water. Transfer the spinach to a small bowl and toss with 1 tablespoon of the sesame oil and the sesame seeds.

4. In a large skillet, heat 2 tablespoons of the vegetable oil over medium heat Carefully crack the eggs into the pan, making sure to keep them far apart. Fry the eggs until the whites are set but the yolk is still runny, 2 to 3 minutes. Transfer the eggs to a plate and set aside.

RECIPE CONTINUES

KIMCHI STEW WITH PORK AND TOFU (KIMCHI JJIGAE)

SERVES 4 AS PART OF A MULTICOURSE MEAL One of the most well-loved stews in Korea, *kimchi jjigae* is a hearty stew of pork belly and tofu simmered with a spicy kimchi-laced broth. Pork can be replaced with thinly sliced shiitake mushrooms for a vegetarian version. Traditionally, this stew is simmered in a *dolsot* (stone or ceramic bowl), but you can simply cook it in a pot and transfer to serving bowls when it's ready. Serve this with a big mound of steamed rice or the Vegetarian Bibimbap with Brown Rice (page 197).

1 pound pork belly, cut into thin bite-size pieces

2 tablespoons mirin

1/4 teaspoon freshly ground black pepper

1 tablespoon vegetable oil

1 large or 2 medium onions, diced

3 cloves garlic, minced

1 tablespoon minced or grated fresh ginger

1 cup tightly packed kimchi, cut into bite-size pieces

2 cups chicken stock, beef stock, or vegetable broth

1 tablespoon kimchi juice (liquid from a jar of kimchi)

2 tablespoons gochujang

1 tablespoon gochugaru

16 ounces soft or medium-firm tofu, drained and rinsed, cut into bite-size pieces 1/2 inch thick

2 teaspoons sesame oil

1 scallion, thinly sliced

Steamed rice, for serving

1. In a medium bowl, stir together the pork belly, mirin, and black pepper. Allow the pork to marinate for 15 minutes at room temperature.

2. In a heavy-bottomed pot, heat the vegetable oil over medium heat. Sauté the pork belly until it begins to turn golden and some of the fat is rendered out, 3 to 4 minutes. Add the onions, garlic, ginger, and kimchi and sauté until the mixture is fragrant, another 2 minutes.

3. Add the stock, kimchi juice, gochujang, and gochugaru, stirring everything to combine. Bring the mixture to a simmer and simmer uncovered for 10 to 15 minutes to reduce the broth slightly. Add the tofu and simmer for another 2 to 3 minutes. Stir in the sesame oil. Divide into individual bowls, garnish with the scallions, and serve with the rice.

GOCHUJANG AND MAPLE ROASTED DELICATA SQUASH

SERVES 4 TO 6 AS A SIDE DISH Delicata squash is one of the easiest winter squashes to roast since it doesn't require peeling. I mix the nutty and earthy gochujang with a bit of maple syrup to coat the squash before roasting. I will often just snack on this like candy, though it also makes a standout fall and winter side dish.

2 tablespoons olive oil

2 tablespoons gochujang

1 tablespoon maple syrup

1 tablespoon sesame oil

2 medium delicata squash
    (about 1½ pounds each)

1 tablespoon toasted white
    sesame seeds

2 scallions, thinly sliced

1. Preheat the oven to 350°F. Line a rimmed baking sheet with parchment paper.

2. In a small bowl, whisk together the olive oil, gochujang, maple syrup, and sesame oil.

3. Slice the delicata squash in half lengthwise and scoop out the seeds. Cut into ½-inch-thick crescents. Place the squash in a large bowl and toss with the gochujang mixture until well coated. Spread the squash in a single layer on the lined baking sheet.

4. Roast until tender and golden brown on top, 20 to 25 minutes. Top with toasted sesame seeds and scallions and serve.

KIMCHI, PAGE 191

Beer

When you're thinking of drinks to go with spicy food, a cold and refreshing beer may be the first thing that comes to mind. Yet you don't want to reach for just any beer; drinking the wrong kind can actually spread heat around your mouth faster, leading to a tear-inducing experience!

"Many people gravitate toward IPAs for a fiery-food pairing, since the bitterness can fan the flames. If you're going the hop route, look for a lower-alcohol IPA, perhaps one that emphasizes the fruity, tropical and citrusy nature inherent in so many hot peppers," says Joshua M. Bernstein, author of *The Complete Beer Course* and *Complete IPA*. He also recommends peppery saisons, Vienna lagers, or caramelly amber ales. "Their malt richness meets the heat head on, and the beers are sturdy enough not to be incinerated by a four-alarm burn."

For something on the lighter side, there are always the good old standbys: Asian-style lagers like Singha or Sapporo. They may be boring to some, but the neutral flavor profiles don't clash with complex flavors. Because starchy foods like rice are also good at neutralizing heat, Bernstein also points out that "the addition of rice in many Asian-style lagers makes them crisp and quenching."

Wine

There is no universal wine that goes with all spicy Asian food, so consider the flavors and nuances of the dishes you'll be eating to choose the best pairing. According to wine writer Hrishi Poola, the rule of thumb is to avoid big, bold, tannic reds and any oaky wines as they may clash with chili flavors and come off as harsh and bitter.

Instead, for white wines to go with Thai, Sichuan, or Indonesian, he recommends off-dry wines with fruit and citrus flavors, such as zesty and gingery Grüner Veltliner from Austria, or for slightly sweeter dishes, Gewürztraminer from Alsace with its bold lychee notes. Sauvignon Blanc, Riesling, and Pinot Gris are also fantastic matches. The hint of fruit or sweetness helps balance out hot and sour flavors, and the citrus notes bring out the herbal and tangy flavors in the dishes, much like if you squeeze lemon over a dish to accentuate flavors.

And don't think you need to stick to white wine. Young red wines such as Zinfandel can be served chilled, and with its hints of star anise and white pepper, make it a refreshing pairing for Chinese food. Full-bodied reds can withstand heavier sauces, but avoid anything high in tannins, which can accentuate bitterness. The smoky and earthy flavors in Tempranillo, Malbec, and Côtes du Rhône can be a fantastic match for Sichuan and Korean dishes.

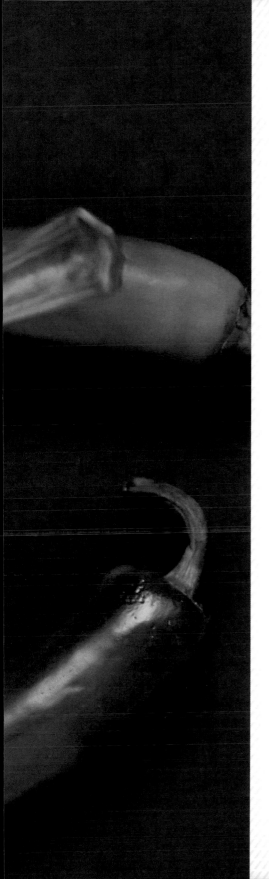

YUZU
KOSHO

YUZU KOSHO AND FRIED EGG AVOCADO TOAST

SERVES 2 I love using yuzu kosho to spice up avocado toast. Whether you enjoy this for breakfast, lunch, or a late-afternoon snack, the citrus-and-jalapeño addition adds a kick to creamy avocado and eggs. For the base, I love using sliced sourdough because of the texture and flavor, but you can use any large slices of bread that will fit a fried egg and arugula.

1 avocado

1 tablespoon yuzu kosho

2 tablespoons vegetable oil

2 large eggs

¼ teaspoon salt

2 slices sourdough bread, toasted

½ cup arugula

½ teaspoon toasted white sesame seeds

1. Halve and pit the avocado and scoop it into a bowl. Mash with a fork until it is still slightly chunky, then mix in the yuzu kosho.

2. In a large skillet, heat the vegetable oil over medium-high heat. Crack each egg into a separate bowl, then once the oil is hot enough, carefully pour the eggs into the pan, making sure the eggs do not touch (if you're using a smaller skillet, cook the eggs in separate batches). After 1 minute, reduce the heat to medium so the bottoms get crisp without overbrowning while the egg yolks are still setting. Cook for another 2 to 3 minutes to your desired level of doneness. (If the egg whites around the yolk are taking a while to set, use a fork to poke holes around the outside of the yolks. This way, the uncooked egg whites on top can seep through, make contact with the pan, and get cooked.) Sprinkle the salt on top.

3. Top off each toast with arugula and a fried egg. Sprinkle the sesame seeds over the eggs and serve.

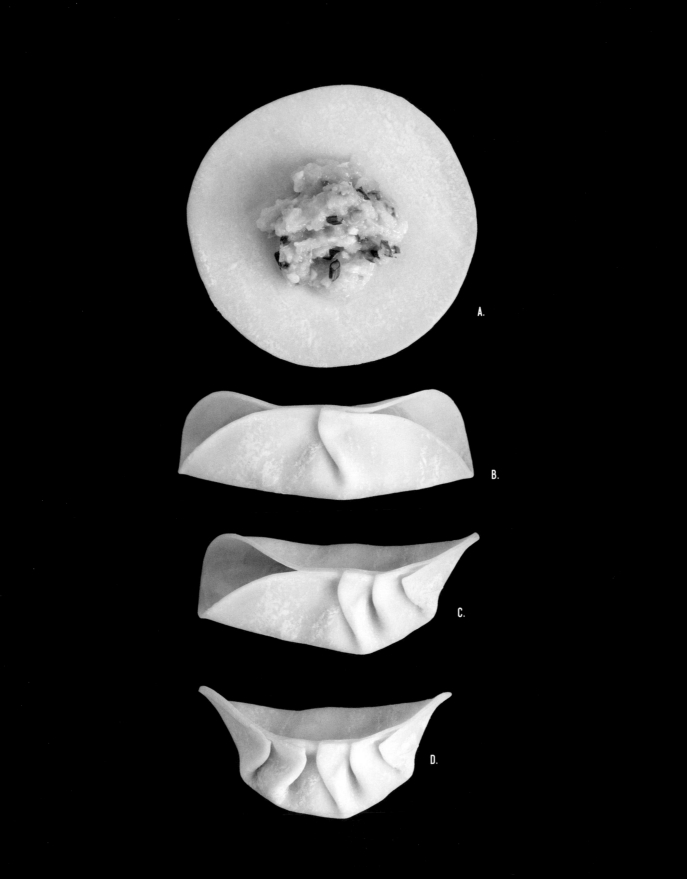

A.

B.

C.

D.

YUZU KOSHO AND GINGER CHICKEN GYOZA

MAKES ABOUT 50 GYOZA If you're already a dumpling or gyoza addict, try this spicy version with chicken, ginger, and yuzu kosho. Folding these little crescent-shaped morsels may seem intimidating at first, but you can follow the step-by-step photographs on the facing page for the secrets to perfect pleating. Take your time practicing. Japanese gyoza wrappers (3½ inches in diameter or smaller) are smaller and thinner than Chinese dumpling wrappers (closer to 4 inches in diameter). If you use Chinese dumpling wrappers, you can use a bit more filling, but add another 1 to 2 minutes to the cooking time.

1 pound ground chicken

2 scallions, finely chopped

1 tablespoon grated fresh ginger

3 tablespoons yuzu kosho

3 tablespoons mirin

2 teaspoons sesame oil

1 package (about 50) gyoza wrappers (or use thin Chinese dumpling wrappers)

2 tablespoons high-temperature vegetable oil, for pan-frying (about 1 tablespoon per dozen)

Soy sauce or tamari, for serving

1. In a large bowl, mix together the chicken, scallions, ginger, yuzu kosho, mirin, and sesame oil.

2. Keep the extra wrappers covered with a slightly damp towel until ready to use, to prevent them from drying out. Fill a ramekin or small bowl of water and have it next to you; this will be for sealing the gyoza. Take a wrapper and place 1 heaping teaspoon of filling in the middle (see a). Be careful not to put in too much or else it will leak out during the folding process.

3. Dip your finger in the water and moisten the edges all around. Take the gyoza in your hand and fold the wrapper in half. With your right thumb and index finger, pinch the edge of the wrapper in the middle and make a pleat (see b). Make 2 more identical pleats in the same direction, until you end up with 3 pleats

on the right side (see c). With your left thumb and index finger, make 2 more pleats on the left side. Press all the pleats to seal. The finished wrapped gyoza should resemble a crescent (see d).

4. Lay the finished gyoza on a plate. Keep the finished gyoza covered with a slightly damp towel while you repeat the process with the remaining gyoza. (If you choose to not pan-fry all your gyoza at once, you can freeze them. Place them in a single layer on a plate lined with parchment paper; they can touch but not overlap. Place them in the freezer for 2 hours, until fully frozen, then transfer them to a freezer bag or other storage container. This way, they pull apart very easily. You can also cook them straight out of the freezer; just add 1 minute more to the steaming time.)

RECIPE CONTINUES

GRILLED MEXICAN CORN (ELOTES) WITH YUZU KOSHO

SERVES 4 One of the best discoveries I made when working on this book was how well yuzu kosho pairs with Mexican food. The flavors of green chilies and limes made yuzu kosho a fantastic ingredient for tacos, guacamole, and sopa de lima. Recently, I tried making elotes (Mexican grilled street corn) with some yuzu kosho in the Mexican *crema* mix. *Elotes* are traditionally cooked on an open grill, but you can also roast the corn in the oven. Cotija, a hard cow's milk cheese that is easily crumbled, is the best to use for the corn, but you can also use ricotta salata or Parmesan for a nuttier salted cheese similar to Mexican Cotija, or use feta for a softer cheese that is similar to US-made Cotija.

3 tablespoons Mexican crema (or mayonnaise)

1 tablespoon yuzu kosho

Vegetable oil, for the grill (optional)

4 ears corn, shucked

1/2 cup finely crumbled Cotija, ricotta salata, Parmesan, or feta cheese

1/2 teaspoon cayenne pepper

2 limes, cut into wedges, for serving

1. If you're grilling, preheat a grill to medium-high. If you're roasting, preheat the oven to 400°F and line a roasting pan or baking sheet with foil or parchment paper.

2. In a small bowl, stir together the crema and yuzu kosho.

3. If grilling, brush the grates with some oil. Grill the corn, turning occasionally, until cooked through and lightly charred, 7 to 8 minutes. If roasting, roast for 25 to 30 minutes (depending on the size of the cobs), until heated through, turning the cobs over about halfway through.

4. Allow the corn to rest for 2 to 3 minutes, then slather all over with the yuzu kosho/crema mixture. Sprinkle the crumbled cheese and cayenne on top and serve with lime wedges for squeezing.

YUZU KOSHO SOBA SALAD

SERVES 4 Cold noodle salads make convenient meals year-round, but are especially great in the summer when longer cooking times seem unbearable. Soba noodles are fantastic because they cook in just 3 to 4 minutes, and the rest of these salad ingredients can be eaten raw. Wakame is a type of seaweed most commonly found in miso soup, but can be simply rehydrated and tossed in a salad. It expands quite a bit when soaked in water, so you need only a handful of dried wakame for four servings. The yuzu kosho dressing has only a few ingredients to allow the chili and citrus flavor of the hot chili paste to shine through.

2 tablespoons yuzu kosho

2 teaspoons honey

2 tablespoons olive oil

1 tablespoon sesame oil

1 tablespoon soy sauce or tamari

2 teaspoons rice vinegar

1 small handful dried wakame

8 ounces soba noodles

2 cups chopped kale, stems discarded, center ribs reserved for another use

1 small bunch red radishes, washed, trimmed, and thinly sliced

2 medium carrots, cut into matchsticks

1 cup soybean sprouts

1 tablespoon sesame seeds, for garnish

2 scallions, thinly sliced or shredded

1. In a small bowl, whisk together the yuzu kosho, honey, olive oil, sesame oil, soy sauce, and rice vinegar.

2. Soak the wakame in a large bowl of water until softened, 10 to 15 minutes. Squeeze the water from the seaweed, roughly chop any pieces that are bigger than bite-size, and set aside.

3. Bring a pot of water to a boil and cook the soba noodles according to package instructions. Drain and rinse the soba under cold water. In a large bowl, toss the soba with half of the yuzu kosho dressing.

4. Toss the soba with the kale, radishes, carrots, bean sprouts, seaweed, and the remaining dressing. Top with the sesame seeds and scallions and serve.

SPICY FISH TACOS WITH YUZU KOSHO SLAW

SERVES 4 The citrus and green chili flavors in yuzu kosho make the zesty Japanese chili paste a wonderful, if slightly unorthodox, ingredient for fish tacos. I like to throw together a slaw flavored with yuzu kosho, mayo, and rice vinegar to serve on warm corn tortillas with the pan-seared fish (which can also be grilled if you'd like to make these for an outdoor cookout). Pair these tacos with the Grilled Mexican Corn (Elotes) with Yuzu Kosho (page 221) for a Japanese-Mexican feast.

SLAW

2 cups shredded red cabbage

1 medium carrot, grated

3/4 cup Japanese or regular mayonnaise

3 tablespoons yuzu kosho

1 tablespoon rice vinegar

1/4 teaspoon salt

TACOS

16 corn tortillas

1 pound firm white fish fillets, such as cod, tilapia, mahimahi, or snapper

3 tablespoons olive oil

1 teaspoon ground cumin

1 teaspoon ancho or chipotle chile powder

1/2 teaspoon salt

1/4 teaspoon freshly ground black pepper

2 avocados, thinly sliced

Cilantro, roughly chopped, for garnish (optional)

2 to 3 limes, cut into wedges, for serving

1. Make the slaw: In a large bowl, combine the cabbage and carrot. In a small bowl, whisk together the mayonnaise, yuzu kosho, rice vinegar, and salt. Pour the mixture over the cabbage mixture and toss to coat. Set aside.

2. Preheat the oven to 300°F.

3. For the tacos: Wrap the tortillas in 4 stacks of 4 tortillas each in foil. Warm the tortillas in the oven for 15 to 20 minutes.

4. When you're ready to cook, lay the fish fillets on a clean work surface and brush 1 tablespoon of the olive oil over the top. Sprinkle evenly with the cumin, ancho powder, salt, and black pepper.

5. Heat a nonstick skillet over medium heat. Working in batches, add 1 tablespoon of olive oil per batch and swirl to coat the bottom. Add the fish fillets and sear until lightly golden on the bottom, 3 to 4 minutes. Carefully flip the fillets and sear on the second side until the fish is opaque and cooked through and flakes off easily with a fork, another 2 to 3 minutes. Transfer to a plate and cover with foil to keep warm while you sear the remaining fish.

5. On a clean work surface, use a fork to shred the fish fillets. Lay out the tortillas in 8 stacks of 2 each (doubling up the corn tortillas makes each taco sturdier). Divide the fish, yuzu slaw, and avocado slices to make 8 tacos. Top with cilantro (if using) and serve with limes for squeezing.

MUSHROOM AND TOFU UDON WITH YUZU KOSHO

SERVES 2 Udon is often a fairly minimalist noodle soup, which makes it an ideal base to taste the flavors of your homemade yuzu kosho. The mushrooms and miso in the vegetable broth give this plenty of savory depth for a vegan noodle soup, but you can also add chicken, shrimp, or other proteins to suit your liking.

1 tablespoon vegetable oil

6 fresh shiitake mushrooms, stems discarded and caps cut in half

4 cups vegetable broth

2 tablespoons yuzu kosho, plus more (optional) for serving

1 tablespoon yellow miso

2 tablespoons soy sauce

2 tablespoons mirin

Two 6-ounce packages fresh udon noodles, or 6 ounces dried udon noodles

6 ounces extra-firm tofu, cut into 1-inch cubes

1/2 cup snow peas, trimmed

4 ounces enoki mushrooms, roots trimmed

2 cups chopped napa cabbage

1 tablespoon sesame oil

2 scallions, thinly sliced

1. In a small skillet, heat the vegetable oil over medium heat. Add the shiitake mushrooms and sauté until golden, 2 to 3 minutes. Transfer to a plate and set aside.

2. In a medium pot, combine the broth, yuzu kosho, miso, soy sauce, and mirin and bring to a boil over high heat. Add the udon, reduce to a simmer, and cook for 1 minute for fresh and 6 minutes for dried. Add the tofu, snow peas, enoki mushrooms, and napa cabbage and cook for another 2 minutes. Stir in the shiitake mushrooms and warm for another 30 seconds. Remove from the heat and drizzle in the sesame oil.

3. Divide the soup, noodles, tofu, and vegetables between two large bowls. Top with the scallions and some more yuzu kosho (if using) and serve.

COOLING DRINKS

Eating spicy food is a lot more enjoyable when you can sip on cooling drinks to balance out the heat. In addition to wine and beer (see What Do You Sip with Spicy Food?, page 207), here are a few nonalcoholic drinks that you can make quickly and easily in your kitchen.

AVOCADO COCONUT SHAKES

MAKES 2 DRINKS This refreshing treat was inspired by the avocado shakes of Vietnam and Indonesia, where avocados grow in abundance and are often blended into creamy, icy concoctions to beat the tropical heat. The avocado shakes in both countries, though, are incredibly thick and sweet—the Indonesian version even has chocolate syrup! So I decided to make a thinner version fit for easy sipping. Yogurt and coconut milk are also remarkable at neutralizing the heat of chilies on your tongue.

1 large avocado

1 cup Greek yogurt

1 cup unsweetened coconut or soy milk

1 cup ice cubes or crushed ice

3 tablespoons honey or agave syrup

Halve and pit the avocado and scoop the flesh into a blender. Add the yogurt, coconut milk, ice, and honey. Pulse, then blend until smooth. Pour into two glasses and serve cold.

AVOCADO COCONUT SHAKES

MAKES 2 DRINKS   This refreshing treat was inspired by the avocado shakes of Vietnam and Indonesia, where avocados grow in abundance and are often blended into creamy, icy concoctions to beat the tropical heat. The avocado shakes in both countries, though, are incredibly thick and sweet—the Indonesian version even has chocolate syrup! So I decided to make a thinner version fit for easy sipping. Yogurt and coconut milk are also remarkable at neutralizing the heat of chilies on your tongue.

1 large avocado

1 cup Greek yogurt

1 cup unsweetened coconut or soy milk

1 cup ice cubes or crushed ice

3 tablespoons honey or agave syrup

Halve and pit the avocado and scoop the flesh into a blender. Add the yogurt, coconut milk, ice, and honey. Pulse, then blend until smooth. Pour into two glasses and serve cold.

TURMERIC-GINGER MILK

MAKES 2 DRINKS For anyone who consumes spicy food in large quantities, it's also important to balance out the heat with detoxifying beverages. Turmeric-ginger tea is one detoxifying drink that can be served either hot or cold. Both turmeric and ginger promote digestion and liver function, while turmeric also reduces inflammation. (On the Japanese island of Okinawa, where residents are reputed to have the longest life expectancies in the world, drinking turmeric tea is a daily ritual!)

This drink is quick and easy to make, but one word of caution: Turmeric tends to stain materials such as wood, laminate, and plastic, so be sure to quickly clean countertops and nonmetallic utensils that come in contact with the turmeric.

One 3-inch piece fresh ginger, cut into 4 or 5 slices

3 tablespoons sugar (or less for reduced sweetness)

2 cups unsweetened soy, almond, or coconut milk

1 teaspoon ground turmeric

1. In a medium pot, combine 1 cup of water and the ginger slices and simmer over medium heat for 10 minutes, stirring occasionally. Add the sugar and stir until dissolved. Fish out the ginger and discard.

2. Add the milk and continue to heat over medium-low heat until it steams but is not yet boiling. Add the turmeric and stir until dissolved. Remove from the heat. Serve hot or let it cool to room temperature and refrigerate for 2 to 3 hours to serve chilled. The turmeric-ginger milk will keep in the refrigerator for 2 to 3 days.

SUPPLEMENTAL RECIPES

These recipes for rice and soup stocks are simple techniques to add to your kitchen repertoire.

RECOMMENDED MENUS

Ⓥ = VEGETARIAN

SUMMER COOKOUT

- Sriracha Sweet and Sour Coleslaw Ⓥ, *page 78*
- Spicy Mango and Tofu Summer Rolls Ⓥ, *page 125*
- Grilled Mexican Corn (Elotes) with Yuzu Kosho Ⓥ, *page 221*
- Spicy Fish Tacos with Yuzu Kosho Slaw, *page 225*
- Sriracha Whole-Kernel Cornbread Ⓥ, *page 62*

LUNAR NEW YEAR

- Hakka-Style Stuffed Tofu, *page 170*
- Stir-Fried Rice Cakes with Zucchini, Mushrooms, and XO Sauce (vegetarian-adaptable), *page 179*
- Steamed Fish with Ginger and XO Sauce, *page 175*
- Sichuan Braised Pork and Vermicelli Noodles (Ants Climbing a Tree), *page 146*
- Hot and Sour Cabbage Ⓥ, *page 157*

THAI DINNER PARTY

- Thai–Style Pomelo Salad with Shallots, Mint, and Coconut Ⓥ, *page 85*
- Thai Lemongrass and Prawn Soup (Tom Yum Goong), *page 91*
- Baked Thai Red Curry Fish Cakes (Tod Mun Pla), *page 104*
- Thai Red Curry Mussels, *page 115*
- Drunken Noodles (Pad Kee Mao), *page 95*
- Coconut Granita with Roasted Sweet Chili Cashews Ⓥ, *page 135*

KOREAN FEAST

- Kimchi Deviled Eggs Ⓥ, *page 194*
- Fresh Cucumber Kimchi Ⓥ, *page 193*
- Spicy Beef Bulgogi, *page 201*
- Korean Spicy Chicken and Rice Cake Stir-Fry (Dak Galbi), *page 199*
- Korean Chilled Spicy Noodles (Bibim Guksu) Ⓥ, *page 189*

SICHUAN SUPPER

- Sichuan-Style Peanut Noodles Ⓥ, *page 145*
- Sichuan Cucumber and Radish Salad Ⓥ, *page 159*
- Chongqing Chicken (La Zi Ji), *page 155*
- Smoky Stir-Fried Tofu with Garlic Chives and Yellow Squash Ⓥ, *page 163*
- Red-Cooked Beef with Daikon Radish, *page 151*

LIGHT AND HEALTHY

- Tatsoi and Romaine Salad with Blood Orange and Sweet Chili Dressing Ⓥ, *page 123*
- Spicy Peanut and Ginger Cucumber Cups Ⓥ, *page 47*
- Roasted Sweet Chili and Ginger Salmon, *page 131*
- Tempeh and Green Beans in Sambal Ⓥ, *page 54*
- Coconut Granita with Roasted Sweet Chili Cashews Ⓥ, *page 135*

FAST WEEKNIGHT DINNERS

- Sichuan Cucumber and Radish Salad Ⓥ, *page 159*
- Bon Bon Chicken (Cold Chicken with Cucumbers in Sesame Sauce), *page 153*
- Shanghai Hot Sauce Noodles Ⓥ, *page 69*
- XO Sauce Cashew Chicken, *page 177*
- Sriracha Fried Rice Ⓥ, *page 75*

GAME NIGHT

- Sriracha Lime Garlic Wings, *page 65*
- Sriracha Hummus with Sun-Dried Tomatoes and Toasted Garlic Ⓥ, *page 63*
- Crispy Tofu with Sweet Chili Peanut Sauce Ⓥ, *page 121*
- Gochujang and Asian Pear Baby Back Ribs, *page 195*
- Sriracha Sweet and Sour Coleslaw Ⓥ, *page 78*

TATSOI AND ROMAINE SALAD
WITH BLOOD ORANGE AND
SWEET CHILI DRESSING,
PAGE 123

WHERE TO BUY INGREDIENTS ONLINE

Kalustyan's

foodsofnations.com

Based in New York, Kalustyan's is a great source for dried chilies from around Asia as well as other essentials like tamarind paste, palm sugar, and *doubanjiang*.

Spices Inc.

spicesinc.com

This Michigan-based online shop sells dried Japonés, bird's eye, Thai spur, and serrano chilies, as well as ground spices, Sichuan peppercorns, and dried shiitake mushrooms from many different producers.

Temple of Thai

templeofthai.com

This store sells a variety of Thai and Chinese ingredients, including sauces, noodles, and aromatics.

Amazon

amazon.com

Where else can you buy a seasoned wok, Korean *onggi*, yuzu juice, and dried spur chilies in one transaction? This is my go-to spot for anything I can't find in brick-and-mortar shops or specialty online shops.

THAI
RED CURRY
MUSSELS,
PAGE 115

INDEX

Page numbers in italics refer to photos.